MAXnotes®

D0839277

Homer's

The *Iliad*

Text by
Beth L. Tanis
*(M.A., University of North Carolina
at Chapel Hill)*

Dr. M. Fogiel
Chief Editor

Illustrations by
James Parks

 Research & Education Association

MAXnotes® for
THE *ILIAD*

Copyright © 1999, 1995 by Research &
Education Association. All rights reserved.
No part of this book may be reproduced in
any form without permission of the
publisher.

Printed in the United States of America

Library of Congress Catalog Card Number 98-66195

International Standard Book Number 0-87891-993-7

What MAXnotes® Will Do for You

This book is intended to help you absorb the essential contents and features of Homer's *Iliad* and to help you gain a thorough understanding of the work. The book has been designed to do this more quickly and effectively than any other study guide.

For best results, this **MAXnotes** book should be used as a companion to the actual work, not instead of it. The interaction between the two will greatly benefit you.

To help you in your studies, this book presents the most up-to-date interpretations of every section of the actual work, followed by questions and fully explained answers that will enable you to analyze the material critically. The questions also will help you to test your understanding of the work and will prepare you for discussions and exams.

Meaningful illustrations are included to further enhance your understanding and enjoyment of the literary work. The illustrations are designed to place you into the mood and spirit of the work's settings.

The **MAXnotes** also include summaries, character lists, explanations of plot, and chapter-by-chapter analyses. A biography of the author and discussion of the work's historical context will help you put this literary piece into the proper perspective of what is taking place.

The use of this study guide will save you the hours of preparation time that would ordinarily be required to arrive at a complete grasp of this work of literature. You will be well-prepared for classroom discussions, homework, and exams. The guidelines that are included for writing papers and reports on various topics will prepare you for any added work which may be assigned.

The **MAXnotes** will take your grades "to the max."

Dr. Max Fogiel
Program Director

Contents

> **Each book includes List of Characters, Summary, Analysis, Study Questions and Answers, and Suggested Essay Topics.**

MAXnotes® are simply the best - but don't just take our word for it...

"... I have told every bookstore in the area to carry your MAXnotes. They are the only notes I recommend to my students. There is no comparison between MAXnotes and all other notes ..."
   – *High School Teacher & Reading Specialist,*
   Arlington High School, Arlington, MA

"... I discovered the MAXnotes when a friend loaned me her copy of the MAXnotes for Romeo and Juliet. The book really helped me understand the story. Please send me a list of stores in my area that carry the MAXnotes. I would like to use more of them ..."
   – *Student, San Marino, CA*

"... The two MAXnotes titles that I have used have been very, very, helpful in helping me understand the subject matter reviewed. Thank you for creating the MAXnotes series ..."
   – *Student, Morrisville, PA*

A Glance at Some of the Characters

Achilleus

Odysseus

Menelaos

Paris

Athene

Diomedes

Andromache

Hektor

SECTION ONE

Introduction

The Homeric Tradition

While the *Iliad* is considered by many to be one of the greatest works of literature ever composed, surprisingly little is known of its author. The poet known as "Homer" is shrouded in mystery. Until the eighteenth century, tradition unquestionably held that Homer was a blind poet who told tales of a time long past even in his own day. It has generally been agreed that Homer lived and worked in the city of Smyrna, located in what is now Turkey. The earliest mention of the name "Homer" is in the work of Xenophanes of Colophon, a philosopher who wrote in the sixth century B.C. There are quotations from work attributed to him in the writings of Plato, Aristotle, and Herodotus among others (Vivante, 24). However, historians have been unable to find any hard evidence of his existence, in large part because he lived before the event of written history.

Because of stylistic similarities, it has been proposed that the *Iliad*, the *Odyssey*, and several other minor works were composed by the same poet, known as Homer. By tradition these poems were handed down over many centuries. Who that poet might have been—and whether or not this is even true—is a matter of debate. One theory is that there was a gifted poet named Homer who composed the skeleton of the works, but that the final version is the result of many different poets expanding and editing the poem over time. Another theory is that the *Iliad* represents the work of many poets and as many as 18 separate poems that were compiled into a coherent whole. It could also have been an expansion of one or more shorter poems by the same author. Evidence for these theories is based on certain inconsistencies within the epic, as well as the existence of some of the material elsewhere, indicating that it must have been borrowed.

Other possibilities certainly exist, and the debate will most likely never be resolved. What is certain, however, is that the *Iliad* and the *Odyssey* are among the world's best known and most influential achievements, together forming the base of a tradition that later included Virgil's *Aeneid*, Dante's *Commedia*, Milton's *Paradise Lost*, and many others.

The Genre of the Epic Poem

The *Iliad* is an epic poem and part of the ancient Greek oral tradition. Homer's audience was an illiterate culture, and Homer himself was most likely illiterate. Many critics believe that the composition of the *Iliad* predated any form of writing in the Greek culture. There are some critics, however, who believe that the *Iliad* must have existed in writing, given its length and complexity. It would have been nearly impossible to maintain such a coherent form by oral transmission alone. This does not mean, however, that it existed in the form that we now know it, or that it was accessible to the general public. If writing did exist, it is thought to have been practiced only by a few storytellers. These "Men of Words" would write down their best tales for their own use and to train their apprentices. They would not be seen by anyone else. Because of the enormous effort of writing, these books would become very valuable possessions, and would be passed down from the storyteller to his successor (Murray, 95-96).

The poets themselves were highly regarded by their contemporaries and treated as fellow workers who attempted to bring beauty to life. The purpose of the tales was both to eloquently preserve the history of a people and to entertain. The stories consisted of a mix of common history borrowed from past poets and embellishments added by the poet. Because these poems were delivered orally, they were adapted and elaborated with each telling, and were never the same twice. Whether written or not, the elaborate tales were recited by professional oral poets as entertainment at banquets, festivals, and fairs. It is known, for instance, that the *Iliad* was performed yearly at the Panathenaea in Athens, a great fair held every four years and lasting several days. At this festival, the *Iliad* was performed in relay fashion by many storytellers competing against each other. Each bard would attempt to make his portion of the poem more entertaining than the others. This resulted in some stretching and embellishment of facts. These were permitted as long as the teller did not deviate too far from known history.

A poet would rely on several routine devices to remember the core events of the narrative. These included the following:

1) **Epic Hero**—a virtuous and noble figure, proven in battle, who represents his nation, culture, or race.

2) **Length**—while each episode was designed to be recounted in a single evening, the entire work is quite long.

3) **Lofty Style**—the tone of the work is primarily serious, and the style is exalted—worthy of the subject.

4) **Epic Similes**—the poem contains extended comparisons between one element or character and something foreign to the poem. The simile helps the reader to see the object in a different way, and says a great deal with fewer words than would otherwise be necessary.

5) **Catalogs/Genealogies**—the work usually contains long inventories or catalogs of characters, equipment, or other elements. Also included are elaborate genealogies of major characters, underlying their history and importance.

6) **Supernatural Involvement**—the main action of the work always includes involvement of the gods to either help or hinder the hero.

7) **Invocation**—most poems begin with an invocation to the Muses, or to some other higher power, requesting guidance. One Muse often invoked is Calliope, the Muse of epic poetry. The invocation serves as an introduction to the action that is about to be recounted.

8) *In Medias Res*—it is not uncommon for an epic poem to begin in the middle of the action and proceed to fill in details of events that occurred earlier.

9) **Voyage Across the Sea**—most epic poems include a sea voyage by the hero or other major character. This convention gives the poet an opportunity to test the hero in unfamiliar circumstances.

10) **Trip to the Underworld**—many epics also contain a dangerous visit to the underworld, where the hero gathers advice and information from the dead.

11) **Epic Battles**—another feature is accounts of fantastic battles between individuals or between vast armies.

The mark of a skilled poet was that he could fit his story into the rigid epic format and add his own style to keep the audience interested and entertained. The *Iliad* is nearly ten times longer than what would ordinarily be performed in one sitting. Other than the marathons in Athens, it was most likely performed in pieces, with the poet relating one episode of the whole at each performance. The stories of the best epic poets were passed down from generation to generation. The *Iliad* and the *Odyssey* were passed down as part of the oral tradition until finally a literate culture wrote them down—probably during the sixth century B.C. No other ancient Greek poet has been so completely preserved.

The Greek text of the *Iliad* is written in dactylic hexameter. The rhythm is therefore one stressed syllable followed by two unstressed syllables, with six of these groups to a line. Many phrases, such as "darkness covered his eyes," or "white armed" to describe a woman, are repeated over and over throughout the poem. This rhythm and formulaic phrasing helped the poet remember his tale. The repetition also helped to stress certain points to a listening audience. While they may not have heard something the first time it was said, they were likely to catch it the second or third time. There are many incidents that recur throughout the work as well, such as the sending of messengers, the assembly of forces, arming for battle, friends avenging the death of friends, and feasting. The effect of all of these techniques in the *Iliad* is a remarkable coherence and unity that far surpasses most epic poems of the same period.

Homer's work differs from many epic poems in another significant way. The subject of the vast majority of these poems involves men possessing supernatural power, serving some higher purpose or fulfilling a mission. They are larger than life in their scope. The *Iliad*, however, is marked by the distinct absence of these devices. The action takes place in the span of days rather than months or years; the gods do interact with the mortals, yet they simply encourage existing possibilities rather than intervening in supernatural ways; the action is full of heroes, yet there is no exaggerated heroism. The result is a perception of the immediate rather than the eternal; a humanizing of the myth. We see the suffering and falling of real men and women rather than of superhuman heroes who are not at all like us. While nearly all of Homer's characters are heroes, they have their moments of weakness and fear as well as moments of great confidence. It has been suggested that this strong focus on purely human experience represents the first instance of art for art's sake, rather than art that served the larger purpose of myth or religion (Vivante, 134).

The History and Culture of Troy

The epic theme Homer chose for the *Iliad* was the Trojan War. At the time the poem was composed, the Trojan War was most likely several centuries past. The poet was safe to assume that his audience was familiar with the major events and myths of the war. Homer could then pick up the action toward the end of the war, and allude only briefly to crucial episodes that occurred earlier. In fact, while the Greek translation of the title is "the poetry about Troy," the actual subject of the epic is the experience of Achilleus, and the action takes place in a period measured in weeks or months. Homer tells us in the *Iliad* that the war has been raging for ten years as his story begins. Historically speaking, this is unlikely. The limited knowledge available through archaeological and cultural research supports a war at Troy lasting only a few years at most.

What we do know of the actual history of the Trojan War is less colorful and far less detailed than the myth. Scholars have argued that the setting of the *Iliad* should not be Asia Minor, but the Greek mainland, where there is evidence that a protracted siege took place in the early Mycenaean Age. It is widely believed that the events of the *Iliad* historically represent a large catalog of ruin throughout the geographical area rather than a single city's destruction. This theory helps to explain Homer's ten years of conflict. Sometime between 1400 B.C. and 1180 B.C., mass destruction occurred on both sides of the Aegean Sea, ravaging much of the Mycenaean world. The period between 1100 and 900 B.C. was a time of mass migration, as survivors of destroyed cities wandered as refugees to Athens, Asia Minor, and the islands of the Aegean. This ruination was one of the greatest disasters the world has known, and would surely be remembered.

This theory also explains some of the unusual customs found in the *Iliad*. For example, burning the dead is contrary to the normal Greek practice of burying them. However, the worst insult imaginable at this time was defilement of a corpse. This is evident throughout the *Iliad* in the many examples of threatened mutilation and throwing bodies to the dogs. In an age when it might be necessary to flee from an invader at any time, one could never be sure that the buried bodies would be safe from defilement by barbaric warriors. It made more sense, therefore, to burn the bodies. When a body is burned, there is nothing left to be defiled. It simply ceases to exist. The elaborate funeral rituals accompanying the burning are an opportunity for the living to symbolically go with the deceased on his journey to the Underworld. Mourners refuse food and water, cut their hair, and remain dirty to show their devotion and willingness to suffer. The funeral games accompanying the death of a hero are meant to allow the living to redefine the social order without the dead man. They compete for glory in the games just as the dead warrior competed for glory on the battlefield. The winners receive valuable possessions that the hero had won in battle, and thus win glory for themselves.

The warriors of the *Iliad* are bound by the heroic code which dictates their behavior in all aspects of social interaction. Above all else, the hero valued his honor. Honor was judged to a great extent by strength in battle, but also to a large degree by adherence to the heroic code. The code is evident many times in battle, as pacts of friendship several generations old are honored in the midst of great carnage. Also, we constantly see warriors avenging the deaths of their companions. The code is also evident in examples of the "guest-host" relationship, in which certain hospitality and behavior is expected. It has been suggested that the real reason Menelaos wages war on Troy is not so much because of the disappearance of his wife Helen, but because Paris so flagrantly violated his responsibilities as a guest in the house of the Achaian. One of the effects of such a code is to encourage conformity and an ordered society. Such unity is essential during battle as each man counts on his fellow warriors to cover him and to avenge him should he die. Paris represents a violation of the social order of Troy. Likewise, while Achilleus is angry with Agamemnon, he is acting as an individual removed from society. A large part of his ultimate transformation will involve his renewed participation in the community and a restored sense of social order.

While the *Iliad* encompasses only a very short episode of a much longer war, the audience would have been familiar with a great deal more of the background than Homer provides. This background includes the cause of the war and the events preceding the action of the *Iliad*, as well as the final destruction of Troy and the death of Achilleus. By ignoring the cause and details of this particular war, Homer turns the *Iliad* into a symbol of all wars.

The Legend of the Trojan War

The events leading up to the Trojan War supposedly began with a wedding feast in Troy. The wedding celebrated the marriage of Thetis, who was a goddess, and Peleus, who was a mortal. Eris, the goddess of discord, showed up and left a golden apple inscribed "For the Fairest" with the wedding guests. This soon set off a competition among three of the women—Hera, Athene, and Aphrodite—each of whom felt they deserved the golden apple. In order to avoid judging such a touchy contest, Zeus (king of the gods, and host of the party) chose Paris, the shepherd, to be the judge. Each of the women then presented Paris with a bribe. Hera's bribe was power and a kingdom of his own; Athene's bribe was wisdom and success in battle; Aphrodite's bribe was love—the love of Helen of Sparta, known to be the most beautiful woman in the world. Paris chose love, forever alienating the other two goddesses.

Unfortunately, Helen was already married to King Menelaos. Undeterred, Paris revealed himself as a true prince who had been abandoned at birth by his mother, Hekuba. (Hekuba had been warned that he would eventually be the cause of the destruction of Troy.) Paris then headed for Sparta and wooed Helen, who ran off to Troy with him (or was carried off to Troy, depending on which version you read). Of course Menelaos was not pleased when he returned to find Helen missing. He gathered together a group of men and a thousand ships to attack Troy and bring Helen back to Sparta. Hence, Helen's was "the face that launched a thousand ships."

When the army reached Troy, it was faced with the enormous wall surrounding the city. The wall had been built with the help and protection of Poseidon (god of the sea). However, the Trojans neglected to pay Poseidon for his help, and he therefore withdrew his protection. Still, it was an impressive wall, and Menelaos' army tried unsuccessfully to penetrate it for ten years. After losing two of their best fighters—Aias and Achilles, the Achaians consulted the "oracles," or fortune-tellers, for advice.

The plan that finally defeated Troy was the famous Trojan horse. The Achaians built a huge wooden horse with room inside for many soldiers. The rest of the army then retreated in their boats, making it look as if they had finally given up. They left one soldier with the task of telling the Trojans that they had left the horse as an offering to please the goddess Athene. According to the story, they were hoping that the Trojans would destroy it, bringing the anger of Athene down on their own heads. The Trojans, seeing that the army was gone, believed the story. They were frightened to anger Athene and so brought the horse inside the city wall. Once inside the walls, the Achaian soldiers waited for darkness. They then came out of the horse and opened the city gates for the rest of the army. Troy was then burned and looted, and only a handful survived the massacre.

Master List of Characters

Achaian Mortals

Achilleus (also called the son of Peleus, or as "of Aiakos' stock")— *Achilleus is the best warrior on the Achaian side. His feud with Agamemnon is central to the plot. Achilleus has the distinct advantage of having been made invulnerable as an infant when his mother submerged him in the River Styx. The only place he is vulnerable is where his mother held him as she dipped him in the water—his heel.*

Agamemnon (also called the son of Atreus)— *Agamemnon, Menelaos' brother, is the king of Mycenae, and Menelaos chooses him to be the leader of the Achaian armies in the campaign against Troy. His feud with Achilleus causes great losses to the Achaian army and is central to the plot.*

Aias (also called the son of Telamon)— *Aias is an elite Achaian warrior, renowned for his courage and strength in battle.*

Aias the Lesser (also the son of Oileus)— *An Achaian warrior.*

Antilochos— *Nestor's son and a brave Achaian warrior.*

Automedon— *Achilleus' chariot driver and squire.*

Briseis— *Briseis was abducted when the Achaians raided Thebes. She was given as a war prize to Achilleus and later taken by Agamemnon.*

Chryseis— *Chryseis is the daughter of Chryses, a priest of Apollo from Thebes. She was abducted as a war prize and given to Agamemnon.*

Diomedes (also called the son of Tydeus)— *An elite Achaian warrior known for his level-headed and courteous manner as well as his skill and bravery in battle.*

Idomeneus— *An Achaian; ruler of Crete.*

Kalchas— *An Achaian prophet.*

Menelaos (also called the son of Atreus)— *King of Sparta and husband of Helen. Menelaos launches the Trojan War in an attempt to revenge himself and to retrieve Helen from Paris, who has run off with her.*

The Myrmidons—*The Myrmidons are the army of Achaian soldiers under Achilleus' command.*

Nestor—*The oldest of the Achaian warriors, and a valuable counselor.*

Odysseus—*One of the elite Achaian warriors renowned for his bravery and strength, Odysseus is chosen by Menelaos to return Chryseis to Thebes.*

Patroklos (also called the son of Menoitios)—*Closest friend of Achilleus and a strong Achaian warrior.*

Thersites—*Obnoxious, insubordinate Achaian.*

Trojan Mortals

Aeneas—*A nobleman, high-ranking in the Trojan army.*

Andromache—*Hektor's wife, who tries to convince him not to return to the fighting.*

Antenor—*A Trojan nobleman who argues that Helen should be returned to Menelaos in order to bring an end to the fighting.*

Antiphos—*Son of Priam and strong Trojan warrior.*

Astyanax—*Son of Hektor and Andromache.*

Cassandra—*Prophetess of Apollo, and daughter of Priam and Hekuba.*

Dolon—*A nobleman of Troy sent out to spy on the Achaian camp. He is captured by Diomedes and Odysseus who are on a similar mission spying on the Trojans.*

Glaukos—*A Trojan prince and warrior.*

Hektor—*Son of Priam and Hekuba, and head of the Trojan armies. Hektor is a responsible and just ruler, as well as the best warrior on the Trojan side.*

Hekuba—*Wife of Priam and mother of Hektor.*

Helen—*Helen is said to be the most beautiful woman in the world. She is the wife of Menelaos, but has run off with Paris, and is living as his wife in Troy.*

Helenos—*A seer, Helenos is another of Priam and Hekuba's sons.*

Idaios—*Herald who urges Priam to make a truce with Agamemnon.*

Pandaros—*Trojan warrior responsible for breaking the truce between the two armies.*

Paris (also known as Alexandros)—*Son of Priam and Hekuba, Paris runs off with Helen, thereby causing the Trojan War. Paris is a coward who is accused many times of shirking his responsibility to fight in the conflict that he caused.*

Poulydamas—*A high-ranking Trojan warrior who gives good advice that is rarely followed.*

Priam (also known as "Dardanian Priam" or "stock of Dardanos")—*King of Troy, husband of Hekuba and father of Paris, Helenos and Hektor. Priam is a good man, and quite old. Legend says that Priam fathered 50 sons and 12 daughters.*

Sarpedon—*Trojan warrior who urges Hektor to rally his troops.*

Teukros—*Achaian warrior who kills many Trojans.*

Gods and Goddesses

Aphrodite (also known as Kypris)—*Goddess of Love, mother of Aeneas and Zeus' daughter, Aphrodite helps the Trojans, and is the champion of Paris.*

Apollo—*Zeus' son, God of Archery, Prophecy, and Poetry. Apollo helps the Trojans.*

Ares—*Son of Zeus and Hera, God of War. Ares helps the Trojans.*

Artemis—*Zeus' daughter, Goddess of Chastity. Artemis helps the Trojans.*

Athene—*Zeus' daughter, Goddess of Wisdom. Athene helps the Achaians.*

Dione—*Aphrodite's mother.*

Hades—*Ruler of the underworld, and God of the Dead.*

Hera—*Zeus' wife and sister who ardently supports the Achaians, sometimes against the wishes of her husband.*

Hermes—*Messenger of the gods, Hermes has links to the underworld and helps the Achaians.*

Iris—*A messenger of the gods.*

Poseidon—*God of the Sea, and Zeus' brother, Poseidon helps the Achaians.*

Paieon—*Healer God who treats Ares' wound.*

Thetis—*Goddess of the Sea, and Achilleus' mother, Thetis beseeches Zeus' aid in revenging the wrong done to her son by Agamemnon.*

Xanthos—*God of a Trojan river, and Zeus' son, Xanthos helps the Trojans.*

Zeus (also called The son of Kronos)—*King of the gods, Zeus' role is the fulfillment of Destiny, and he is not aligned with either side.*

Summary of the Work

Chryses, a priest of Apollo, journeys to the Achaian camp to request the return of his daughter Chryseis. Chryseis had been captured in a Greek siege and given to Agamemnon as a war prize. Chryses has brought many gifts as ransom for his daughter, but Agamemnon refuses to accept them and sends Chryses away. Apollo then revenges the ill treatment shown to his priest by sending a plague to the Greeks. The plague claims many lives, and a counsel is held to determine how to stop it. Through the advice of a seer, the Greeks agree that the return of Chryses is the only way to stop the plague from taking even more lives. Agamemnon, however, does not give up his prize willingly, and insists that he must have another man's prize in exchange. He demands Briseis, the woman given to Achilleus in the same siege. Achilleus is so angry with Agamemnon for taking Briseis that he immediately withdraws himself and his troops from the fighting with Troy. He also asks his mother, the goddess Thetis, to plead with Zeus to help him avenge the wrong. Zeus agrees to assist the Trojans in their attack on the Achaians, thus showing Agamemnon that Achilleus is a great man, who would be necessary to succeed in battle.

Agamemnon gathers the rest of his army for a massive attack against the Trojans. The first day of battle opens with a duel between Paris and Menelaos, and a truce among the rest of the armies. After the duel, which ends with Paris being taken out of the battle by Aphrodite, the truce is broken by Pandaros, the Trojan, and the two armies engage in bitter fighting. At the end of the day, there is another duel, this time between Aias and Hektor, which is broken up before its end. The two sides retreat, and the Achaians build a wall around their encampment to protect their position and their ships.

When fighting resumes, Zeus pushes the Trojans to great triumph over the Achaians, and their victory seems certain. At this point, Agamemnon calls his leaders together and admits he was at fault in taking Briseis from Achilleus. He agrees to return her, along with a great deal of treasure and a sworn oath that he has not slept with her, if Achilleus will come back and fight with the Achaians. The message is brought to Achilleus by his good friends Odysseus, Aias, and Phoinix. Achilleus greets his friends warmly, but refuses to make peace with Agamemnon.

The next day the fighting resumes, and the Achaians fight well. However, over the span of the day, most of the best men are injured and taken out of the fight. These include Agamemnon, Diomedes, Odysseus, Eurypylos, and Machaon. The only remaining champion of the Achaians is Aias. Hektor then leads a strong drive by the Trojans, and they manage to break through the Achaian wall and fight all the way to the ships. As the Trojans attempt to set fire to the Achaian ships, the gods intervene and rescue the Achaians from almost certain destruction. At this point, Achilleus and his companion Patroklos become fearful for the fate of the Achaian army. While Achilleus still refuses to fight, he sends Patroklos out to the field in his own armor with a contingent of men to save the ships.

Because Patroklos and his army are rested and fresh, they easily drive the weary Trojans back to the city wall. Patroklos fights bravely and performs many courageous acts, but he pushes his luck and is eventually killed by Hektor. Hektor takes the famous armor of Achilleus from Patroklos, and a fierce battle is fought over his body. The Achaians manage to retrieve the body of Patroklos, but the battle has turned to the Trojan's favor, and the Achaians retreat. When Achilleus hears the news of his companion's death, he is mad with rage against Hektor, but cannot rush into the battle without his armor. However, the gods transfigure him and when he shows himself on the battlefield the Trojans pull back and the Achaians escape. His mother Thetis acquires immortal armor from the god Hephaistos, and Achilleus announces to the assembled Achaians the end of his quarrel with Agamemnon. The next day the Achaians, mostly through the exploits of Achilleus, are able to drive the Trojans back inside their city walls. Hektor, however, refuses to go inside, promising to encounter Achilleus directly instead. His courage fails at the last minute and Achilleus pursues Hektor twice around the city walls. Hektor's flight is finally halted through the trickery of Athene, and the two men duel. Hektor is killed and his body is dragged by the ankles behind Achilleus' chariot back to the Achaian camp.

Achilleus then holds funeral games for Patroklos, giving many great prizes to the victors. Patroklos' body is mourned and burned in a great pyre. In his grief over his friend, Achilleus has been dishonoring the body of Hektor, but the gods have kept it from mutilation. Priam is secretly guided by the gods to Achilleus to request his son's body in exchange for a great ransom. Achilleus has pity on him, and returns the body. The Trojans then bury Hektor.

Estimated Reading Time

Allow an hour or slightly more to read each chapter, or book. There are a total of 24 books in the *Iliad*, totaling roughly 24-26 hours of reading time. **Note:** This MAXnotes book is based on the 1951 Richmond Lattimore translation of the *Iliad*.

The *Iliad*

Book One

New Characters:

Achilleus: *greatest warrior of the Achaian army*

Agamemnon: *head of the Achaian army against Troy*

Chryses: *priest whose daughter was abducted as a war prize by the Greeks*

Chryseis: *Theban woman given to Agamemnon as a war prize*

Kalchas: *seer who offers advice*

Athene: *goddess who restrains Achilleus from slaying Agamemnon*

Nestor: *old Achaian warrior who offers advice*

Odysseus: *one of Agamemnon's counselors*

Talthybios: *herald and servant of Agamemnon*

Eurybates: *herald and servant of Agamemnon*

Briseis: *Theban woman given to Achilleus as a war prize*

Patroklos: *friend of Achilleus*

Menelaos: *brother of Agamemnon, and husband of Helen whose retreat with Paris is the reason for the war*

Thetis: *mother of Achilleus*

Zeus: *king of the gods*

Hera: *wife of Zeus*

Hephaistos: *Hera's son; a lame craftsman god associated with fire*

Summary

The *Iliad* begins with the narrator requesting help from his Muse in telling his tale. In this introductory piece, the hero of the epic is "Godlike Achilleus." The plot of the story involves a quarrel between Achilleus and Agamemnon and its disastrous consequences.

One of the many exploits of the Achaian army was the sacking of the city of Thebe. The Achaians brought back the spoils and divided them equally among the warriors. Agamemnon's prize was a maiden named Chryseis. Achilleus' prize was a maiden named Briseis.

Some time later, the father of Chryseis—Chryses—comes to Troy to plead with the Achaians for her return. He brings with him vast amounts of riches to offer as ransom. After Chryses pleads his case, all of the Achaians (except Agamemnon) agree that Chryseis should be returned to her home. Rather than give up his war prize, Agamemnon sends Chryses away with harsh, angry words.

Chryses, a priest of Apollo, prays to his god to avenge the wrong done him by the Achaians. Apollo then sends "deadly arrows," or a great plague, against the Achaians, and many of them are killed. After ten days of this deadly attack, Achilleus calls the Achaians together to discuss what can be done. They ask the advice of Kalchas, a seer. He advises that the only way to stop the bloodshed is to let Chryseis go. Agamemnon is extremely angry. He agrees to give up Chryseis if forced to, but only if he can have another prize in her place. Achilleus offers to compensate Agamemnon three or four times over when Zeus gives the Achaians the victory over Troy. However, Agamemnon insists that he will take his prize immediately, and that his prize will be Briseis. At this point, Achilleus nearly kills Agamemnon on the spot, but he is restrained by the goddess Athene.

Achilleus is greatly angered by these events which he considers grossly unfair. He pulls his troops out of the battle against the Trojans. After all, Achilleus had no personal stake in the fight with Troy. He was there only to help Menelaos retrieve his wife, Helen, who had run off with Paris. Achilleus announces that he and his army will return to their own land. Agamemnon sends his men to retrieve Briseis from Achilleus' tent. Realizing he has little choice, he lets her go.

Achilleus then meets with his mother, Thetis, goddess of the water, and pours out his tale to her. Achilleus asks her to beseech Zeus for help in his revenge. His plan is to have Zeus aid the Trojans in their fight against the Achaian army, thereby destroying many of them in the fighting. The Achaians will then realize how valuable a warrior Achilleus was to them and repay the wrong done to him. Thetis is moved by her son's anger. She knows that his fate is to die at a young age. Because of this, she agrees to do what she can to make his brief time on earth more bearable. She speaks to Zeus, who reluctantly agrees to aid the Trojans.

Meanwhile, Odysseus has sailed to Thebe to return Chryseis to her father. Along with the girl he has brought 100 oxen to be sacrificed as a peace offering. He is joyfully received, and a great feast is held to celebrate Chryseis' return. The anger of Chryses and Apollo has been appeased.

When Zeus' wife, Hera, discovers what Zeus has promised to Thetis, she is not pleased. She chastises him for agreeing to bring honor to Achilleus at the expense of many Achaian lives. Hera cared for the Achaians when they were dying in Apollo's assault. She also despises the Trojans. Zeus makes it very clear that he is not only her husband, but also the king of the gods, and as such he is not obligated to answer to her for every choice that he makes. Hera's son Hephaistos urges his mother to make peace with her husband. The gods are planning a great feast, and he does not wish it to be spoiled. Hera agrees, and the chapter concludes with the great feast of the gods, and Hera and Zeus sleeping peacefully side by side.

Analysis

Book One opens with the standard epic invocation to the Muse. In this case, the goddess invoked is not named. We can assume, however, that Homer is requesting help in telling his tale from the goddess of poetry. The poet hoped that the Muse would reveal elements of the story that could not be known by normal means. He also requested artistic assistance to render the tale in a beautiful and entertaining manner. We learn in the invocation that "godlike Achilleus" will be the epic hero and that the action will stem from his tremendous anger against the son of Atreus—Agamemnon. We know from this invocation that a very significant part of the action has already occurred. The narrator has employed the epic convention of *in medias res*. We can then expect the narrator to fill in the details of the events that led to Achilleus' great quarrel with Agamemnon.

The example of Chryseis and Briseis is a dire reminder of what will become of the women of Troy should the Achaians succeed in taking Troy. At this time, any warrior who was not killed in battle was kept as a slave or sold into slavery. The women were taken as concubines or wives for the conquering heroes. A warrior who proved himself worthy in battle would receive a larger share of the spoils than a warrior who had been cowardly. As Achilleus showed himself to be the best of the Achaians in combat, he justly deserved a large share of the spoils. Agamemnon is taking treasure that he has not earned. However, it will become clearer as the epic unfolds that the real issue for Achilleus is not treasure. Achilleus is far more interested in honor. When Agamemnon takes Briseis, he is insulting Achilleus and demeaning his position in the social order. Achilleus will come to represent internal values such as spirit and honor. It is Agamemnon who will prove to be far more interested in possessions. Agamemnon will represent external values and place large emphasis on gifts. He will prove again and again to be devoid of substance.

While the anger of Achilleus is justified, his reaction reveals his tragic flaw. Achilleus shows not only anger, but excessive pride. He is certainly the best warrior among the Achaians. His strength and bravery have been proven in many battles. In a society which places the highest value on these assets, Achilleus can rightly claim great honor and deference. It is also true that Agamemnon acted childish when he insisted on taking Briseis. There was cause for both pride and anger. However, when Achilleus removes his forces from the battle, he takes his anger too far. As the epic continues, it will become clear that Achilleus can control neither his pride nor his anger. Eventually, this tragic flaw will lead to a string of disastrous decisions, and finally, death.

The act of Achilleus withdrawing from the Trojan War is the most significant event of Book One. This single act will propel the plot throughout the epic. Achilleus has agreed to fight to help Menelaos recover Helen. His quarrel here, however, is not with Menelaos, but with Agamemnon, who has been put in charge of the Achaian forces. The tone of the first chapter leads us to believe this action will have dire consequences. In fact, the narrator describes the results of Achilleus' anger as bringing "uncounted anguish on the Achaians" as a result of "Zeus' will." In asking Zeus for help in his revenge, Achilleus will bring great tragedy to the Achaians.

We also know from Book One that it is Achilleus' fate to die young. Knowing that Achilleus has already made a name for himself in battle, and that he commands a good-sized army, we can assume that his own demise is not far off. The events of this introductory chapter set up the machinery that will lead inevitably to his death. The theme of mortality is strong throughout the epic, and Achilleus is only one example. In a war-loving society where glory comes on the battlefield, the characters are constantly aware that they could face their death at any time. Because of this awareness, they attempt to perform great feats of battle that will be talked about long after they have died. In this way they achieve a degree of immortality.

The large role of the gods is also established in Book One. The first major encounter with the gods involves the wrath of Apollo. Agamemnon's actions lead directly to retaliation by Apollo on Chryses' account. The gods are not distant supreme beings remote from human life. They are very much involved with the actions of mortals. Achilleus' plan to win greater glory for himself by withdrawing from the action and then enlisting the help of the gods to assist the Trojan forces escalates the conflict with Agamemnon. By enacting this plan, Achilleus has broadened the action to include not only all of the Trojan and Achaian armies, but also the entire range of gods. As the gods choose sides, assisting either the Trojans or the Achaians, the immortal action mirrors that of the mortals on the battlefield.

The gods, however, are not remote supernatural beings who control the circumstances on earth. Instead they are greatly humanized, experiencing the whole range of human emotions. Zeus and Hera experience the same bickering and emotions as a mortal married couple. They also engage in the very human activities of feasting and sleeping. Throughout the epic, the gods will be vitally involved in the action. While there are many offerings and sacrifices made to the gods, they do not need to be summoned by prayer. They are present spontaneously, encouraging men to act. At the same time, the gods seem to be vitalized by men. Gods and men are interdependent to a large degree.

Study Questions

1. Where are the Achaians at the opening of the epic?

2. Why did Apollo send "deadly arrows" against the Achaians?
3. Whose advice do the Achaians seek to stop the bloodshed?
4. What do the Achaians do to stop Apollo's assault?
5. What does Agamemnon do to Achilleus that causes his great anger?
6. What is Achilleus' plan for revenge?
7. Why does Thetis agree to help Achilleus?
8. Who takes Chryseis back to Thebe, and what happens when he gets there?
9. Why is Hera unhappy that Zeus agrees to help Achilles?
10. Who pleads with Hera to make peace with Zeus, and why?

Answers

1. The Achaians are in Troy.
2. The Achaians refused to return Chryseis to her father, who is a priest of Apollo.
3. The Achaians seek the advice of Kalchas, a seer.
4. The Achaians return Chryseis to Thebe.
5. Agamemnon takes Achilleus' war prize, Briseis.
6. Achilleus plans for the gods to assist Troy in their fight against the Achaians.
7. Thetis is Achilleus' mother. She also knows that Achilleus' fate is to die young.
8. Odysseus takes Chryseis back to Thebe, and everyone celebrates with a feast.
9. Hera thinks it unfair that many of the Achaians must die to revenge Achilleus. She also despises the Trojans and does not want them to win the war.
10. Hera's son, Hephaistos, pleads with his mother to make peace with Zeus so as not to spoil their great feast.

Suggested Essay Topics

1. Compare the actions of Achilleus to those of Agamemnon in this chapter. What do these actions tell you about each of the characters?

2. Examine the role of women in this chapter. How are the women treated? How do they effect the action? Is the role of the goddesses different from that of the mortals?

Book Two

New Characters:

Thersites: *obnoxious, insubordinate Achaian*

Iris: *messenger goddess sent by Zeus to warn Trojans of attack*

Summary

Book Two opens with Zeus' plan to aid Achilleus in his revenge. Zeus sends Agamemnon the message that the gods are now on the Achaian side, and that they will be victorious in their campaign against Troy. To convey the message, Zeus sends Dream in the form of Nestor.

Agamemnon wakes from his dream convinced that the Achaians will now defeat Troy. At the same time, Zeus sends his messenger Rumour among the armies to urge them on to battle. The armies are called together and Agamemnon tests them by telling them to give up and go home. To his surprise, the men are overjoyed and cheer loudly as they race to the ships that will take them home.

However, Hera is not pleased with this reaction, and she sends Athene down to urge the men back to the fight. Athene reminds Odysseus of the many men already dead, and how pointless their deaths will be if the cause is not won. Odysseus then takes Agamemnon's scepter and urges the men back to the battle, egging them on with taunts of their weakness and cowardly nature. Eventually the prodding is rewarded, and the troops turn back. However, one warrior, Thersites, refuses to listen to Odysseus' rea-

soning. He insults and taunts Agamemnon and argues for abandoning him in Troy. When Odysseus rebukes him and beats him with the scepter, all of the armies applaud. Thersites has no defenders.

Odysseus urges the armies to stay and fight, reminding them of the sign they received before taking on the cause. A snake devoured eight sparrow chicks and then the mother sparrow before turning to stone. Then Nestor addresses the assembly, reminding the men of the pledges they had made to the cause and of the lightning seen on the right side of the boats as they sailed to Troy, signifying victory. The men are convinced to stay.

Agamemnon then calls the men to battle and they disperse to prepare, sacrificing to the gods and praying that they will escape

death in the coming battle. Athene circulates among the men rais-
ing their strength for the fight. The narrator then gives us a long
list of the army divisions of the Achaians. Indicated here are the
leader of each army, the land they are from, and how many ships
they brought with them to Troy.

The messenger goddess Iris is sent to the Trojans to warn them
of the Achaian attack. The Trojan army and its allies prepare for
battle and exit the city gate to fight, led by Hektor. The chapter ends
with a list of the army divisions fighting for Troy.

Analysis

In Book Two we see two prominent examples of personification: Dream and Rumour. Zeus is said to send his "messengers"
Dream and Rumour in order to accomplish some purpose. The
reader can clearly see that the gods are not just aware of the actions of men, but are constantly manipulating them. When Zeus
sends Dream in the form of Nestor, he consciously chooses the
person that Agamemnon most respects and trusts. Zeus knows that
this increases the possibility of Agamemnon believing and acting
on the message. Similarly, Rumour is sent to disseminate a certain
mood among the troops—to put an idea into their heads. However, while Dream succeeded in convincing Agamemnon of the
message from Zeus, Rumour was apparently unsuccessful in spurring the army on to battle. As soon as they are given the opportunity, they are more than ready to abandon the cause.

A major conflict in this book is presented by Thersites. While
Thersites comes across as being obnoxious and laughable, his ar-
guments are not without merit. The Achaians have been waging
war with Troy for nine years. In nine years they are no closer to
retrieving Helen than they were when they arrived. The average
warrior in the Achaian force has no personal interest in the cause—
only Menelaos does. A lack of commitment to the fight is clearly
shown when Agamemnon tests the warriors and they rush to their
ships to abandon the cause. While it is obvious that Thersites is
unpopular among the men, his outburst is still dangerous.
Odysseus recognizes this and physically suppresses him with
blows. It is important that the armies be united as they go to battle.

Although Agamemnon is completely convinced of victory in

this next battle, we know that Zeus has set him up for failure. Zeus' plan is not to aid Agamemnon, but instead to help the Trojans, thus assisting Achilleus in avenging himself against his enemy. Thersites, the troublemaker, is actually the only one who sees that Agamemnon has acted foolishly. He accuses Agamemnon of waging this war for his own selfish gain. Indeed, we know that Agamemnon's foolishness has already alienated his best warrior, Achilleus. Without Achilleus and his army, the battle will be much more difficult for the Achaians. Thersites points to Agamemnon's weakness as a ruler, which will become more evident as the epic continues.

In the epic catalog at the end of the chapter, the absence of Achilleus' army is ominously noted. The narrator includes this long list to impress on his listeners the size and strength of the armies. Descriptions also include historic information and distinguish the leaders, either by ancestry or by accomplishment. Achilleus is named "by far the strongest," and Aias the best without him. In this way, Homer impresses on the reader the enormity of the loss to the Achaian forces.

Study Questions

1. How does Zeus convey his message to Agamemnon?

2. What is Zeus' message, and can it be trusted?

3. How does Agamemnon test the warriors?

4. Do the warriors pass the test?

5. Which goddesses help to turn the army back to the fight?

6. What is the sign that Odysseus takes as proof of impending victory?

7. Who is the one warrior who refuses to listen to Odysseus, and what is his argument?

8. How does Odysseus react to Thersites?

9. Why does the narrator include a list of the armies with their leaders and ships?

10. How do the Trojans find out about the Achaian attack?

Answers

1. Zeus sends Dream in the form of Nestor to convey his message to Agamemnon.

2. Zeus tells Agamemnon that the Achaians will be victorious against the Trojans. His advice cannot be trusted, because Zeus is helping Achilleus get revenge against Agamemnon.

3. Agamemnon tests the warriors by telling them to give up and go back home.

4. The warriors fail the test, jumping immediately at the opportunity to go home.

5. Hera sends Athene down among the troops to encourage them to fight.

6. The sign Odysseus uses to convince the armies is that of a snake devouring eight baby sparrows and their mother, and then being turned to stone. He tells them this indicates nine years of fighting and then victory.

7. The warrior who dissents is Thersites, and he argues that Agamemnon is fighting only for selfish reasons of personal glory.

8. Odysseus rebukes Thersites verbally, and then beats him with Agamemnon's scepter.

9. The catalog of armies is given to impress the listener with the size of the forces, and also to give some background information on the leaders.

10. Zeus sends the goddess Iris to the Trojans to warn them of the Achaian attack.

Suggested Essay Topics

1. Discuss the various ways that the gods accomplish their purposes with men in this book. Are these methods always successful? What does this say about the ultimate power of the gods in this culture?

2. Discuss the warriors' attitude toward the battle. How does it change throughout this book? Which characters sway their opinions, and what methods are used to convince them?

Book Three

New Characters:

Alexandros (Paris): *abductor of Helen and cause of the war; basically a coward*

Aphrodite: *Goddess of Love and mother of Aneas*

Helen: *wife of Menelaos and mistress of Paris*

Priam: *father of Paris and King of Troy*

Idaios: *herald who urges Priam to make a truce with Agamemnon*

Antenor: *accompanies Priam to make truce with Agamemnon*

Summary

The Trojans and Achaians approach each other to do battle. As they prepare to fight, Alexandros (Paris) challenges the best of the Achaians to a duel. However, when Menelaos agrees to fight, Paris cowardly shrinks back into the ranks. Hektor derides Paris for causing the war and then having no courage to fight. Paris is so shamed by his brother's remarks that he agrees to duel with Menelaos for Helen and all of her goods, leaving the rest of the armies out of it.

The armies are overjoyed with this plan, and quickly lay down their armor and prepare to make a truce. Idaios the herald is sent to summon King Priam, who rides down in his chariot with Antenor to meet Agamemnon and Odysseus. Together they swear that the winner of the fight will keep Helen and all her goods. When the conditions have been met, the Achaians will return to their home. However, if Menelaos wins and Priam refuses to pay, the Achaians will fight the war to its end. Two lambs are sacrificed and everyone prays to Zeus, cursing any who offend the oath.

Hektor and Odysseus then measure out the dueling ground in a large open space between the two armies. Lots are shaken, and Paris draws the honor of throwing the first spear. Soon after the fighting begins, it becomes apparent that Menelaos is the better warrior. After inflicting a small wound, he knocks Paris to the ground and drags him triumphantly by the plume of his helmet to the Achaian onlookers. However, before he reaches his companions, Aphrodite wraps Paris in a thick mist and spirits him away from the battlefield. She deposits him in his bedroom and calls Helen to him.

Agamemnon declares Menelaos the victor of the duel, because he had been winning before Paris disappeared. He calls for the Trojans to give Helen and her possessions back, and to provide compensation. The book ends with the Achaians applauding their leader.

Analysis

In the beginning of this book there is tension between Paris and the Trojans. While Paris was completely and solely responsible for causing the war that has now raged on for nine solid years, he is neither quick to take responsibility nor to do his fair share of the fighting. His act of bravado in challenging the best of the Achaians to a duel reveals his cowardice. Hektor expresses the views of the majority of Trojans when he taunts Paris. After the disappearance during the duel, it states that none of his companions would have hidden him, "since he was hated among them all as dark death is hated" (line 454). Hektor is in an awkward position. As Paris' brother and commander of the forces, Hektor is duty-bound to protect him and to fight for him. However, it is Paris who has brought disruption to the social order of Troy and has put the family at risk. This is a recurring issue in the epic, and Hektor will continually chide Paris for his irresponsible behavior.

The actual duel between Menelaos and Paris over Helen acts as a capsulated version of the entire war. These three characters are, after all, the only ones involved in the original conflict. The duel would therefore seem more appropriate at the beginning of the war, rather than at this point ten years later. Still, we see two strong fighters with the advantage at first shifting sides, then resting decidedly with the Achaian fighter who eventually triumphs. Added to this action is the intervention of Aphrodite, who acts as a symbol of the intervention of the gods in the larger conflict. The outcome of this duel foreshadows the inevitable outcome of the Trojan War.

This chapter also illuminates the conflicting emotions of Helen. Before Priam is called to the battlefield to agree to the truce, he confers with Helen. She gives her father-in-law a description of the key figures in the Achaian army. Throughout the chapter, Helen's allegiances are turned toward the Achaians, and she begins to miss the life she left as wife of Menelaos. As Aphrodite attempts to draw her back to Paris, Helen swears she will never return to his bed. When she is threatened with disaster, Helen agrees to go to Paris, but then tells him she wishes he had died in the duel. Helen realizes that Menelaos is the better man, but knows she must stay with Paris.

Interestingly, while Helen represents the cause of the conflict between the Achaians and the Trojans, she herself is alienated. Paris is weak and cowardly, and she appears to be bored in Troy. Here we see her sympathies shift to Menelaos and her former home, but she is not passionate about that either. The truth is, whether Helen is with Paris or with Menelaos, her situation will not change significantly. She is like a trophy; a thing to be possessed. Yet in reality, no one can own her. She is ruled by Aphrodite, in bondage to the gods, and she goes where they tell her to go. Helen is beauty personified, and beauty deserts those who desire to hold it too tightly.

Study Questions

1. How do the Trojans feel about Paris, and why?
2. What incident in this chapter shows us this feeling?
3. Who reprimands Paris for his behavior?
4. What does Paris eventually agree to do?
5. Where is the duel fought?
6. Who has the upper hand in the fighting?
7. How does the duel end?
8. Who is declared the winner?
9. Is Helen happy to see Paris returned to his room?
10. What does the duel between Paris and Menelaos symbolize?

Answers

1. The Trojans despise Paris because he is directly responsible for the war with the Achaians. He is also a coward who refuses to do his share of the fighting.

2. Paris challenges the best of the Achaian men to a duel, but then backs away in fear when Menelaos accepts it. Also, after he disappears we are told that no one among the Trojans would hide him.

3. Paris' brother Hektor chides him for his behavior.

4. Paris agrees to fight a duel with Hektor to decide the fate of Helen, leaving the rest of the armies out of it.

5. The duel is fought in a large clearing between the two armies.

6. Menelaos is the better fighter.

7. The duel ends when Menelaos has clearly established the upper hand, but before he can finish Paris off, Aphrodite spirits the Trojan away.

8. Agamemnon declares Menelaos the winner, since he was clearly the better fighter.

9. Helen is not happy to see Paris alive, and goes to him only when forced by Aphrodite to do so.

10. The duel is a symbol of the larger conflict between the Achaians and the Trojans.

Suggested Essay Topics

1. Discuss Paris' role in the Trojan conflict. What kind of man is he? Why is Helen unhappy in his presence?

2. Describe Helen and her role. What does she represent, and why is it worth fighting a ten year war over?

Books Four and Five

New Characters:

Pandaros: *the Trojan who breaks the truce by shooting an arrow at Menelaos*

Talthybios: *herald of Menelaos who summons Machaon to heal Menelaos' wound*

Machaon: *healer who treats Menelaos' wound*

Idomeneus: *leader of the Cretan forces who pledges loyalty to Agamemnon*

Diomedes: *one of the strongest Achaian warriors*

Stethenelos: *companion of Diomedes*

Ares: *God of War who helps the Trojans*

Antilochos: *first Achaian to kill a Trojan warrior*

Telamonian Aias: *one of the strongest Achaian warriors*

Antiphos: *son of Priam and strong Trojan warrior*

Hektor: *son of Priam and leader of the Trojan forces*

Apollo: *god who fights on the Trojan side*

Aineias: *son of Aphrodite and counselor to the Trojans, wounded by Diomedes*

Dione: *mother of Aphrodite who heals her wound*

Sarpedon: *Trojan warrior who urges Hektor to rally his troops*

Paieon: *healer god who treats Ares' wound*

Summary

Book Four opens with a meeting of the gods, who discuss the outcome of the duel in the last chapter. Zeus recommends ending the war, as Menelaos was decidedly the winner. However, Hera and Athene are bent on destroying Troy completely, and argue against a truce. In the end, Athene is sent to provoke further fighting.

She accomplishes her goal by persuading Pandaros to gain glory for himself by killing Menelaos. Pandaros takes her advice and shoots an arrow at Menelaos. The arrow reaches its mark and draws blood, but is not fatal. The action produces the desired results, and both sides are stirred to battle. The fighting is fierce, and a great number of soldiers are killed on both sides.

As Book Five opens, the battle is still waging. The center of attention here is Diomedes, who, with help from Athene, performs many courageous acts. When Diomedes is wounded by Pandaros, Athene gives him the advantage of recognizing the gods on the battlefield. She warns him, however, not to engage any of the gods in combat except Aphrodite whom she despises.

Diomedes continues to kill many Trojans, and eventually wounds the son of Aphrodite, Aineias. Aphrodite quickly comes to her son's rescue, leading him out of the battle. Diomedes, however, intent on finishing the job of killing Aineias, chases them and wounds Aphrodite in the hand with his spear. Aphrodite drops her son and runs off to Olympus hurt and frightened. Zeus orders her to stay out of the war as she is not trained in warfare. Apollo then carries Aineias to safety.

The advantage goes back and forth as the gods lend their aid to one side and then the other. At a point when Ares is spurring the Trojans on to the upper hand, Athene and Hera urge Diomedes on and he badly injures Ares with his spear. The God of War angrily leaves the field and heads for Olympus to complain to Zeus. Zeus, however, is not sympathetic, and tells Ares his violent nature led to his wound. The battle on earth continues without help from the gods on either side.

Analysis

At this point in the story, it looks as though the war will end, Helen will be returned to Menelaos, and the Achaians will sail for home. Zeus is concerned for the mortals. However, Hera and Athene have a long-standing grudge against Troy and want to see the city destroyed. The decision of the immortals to encourage further conflict will bring about the deaths of many warriors on both sides.

When Athene chooses Pandaros to break the truce, she knows that he is not incredibly bright. The war has now been raging for nine long years. Both armies are tired of the fighting and eager to return to their families. This became evident in Book One as the Achaians quickly took Agamemnon up on his plan to sail home, and also in the joyful reaction of both sides to settling the matter once and for all with a duel between Paris and Menelaos. Athene chooses Pandaros precisely because she knows she can convince him to go for glory and forget the consequences. If he can kill Menelaos, he knows that his name will live on and he will be a hero of the Trojans. This is an expansion of the theme of mortality versus immortal glory. It is also an example of the gods simply encouraging men to do what they desire to do anyway. Athene does not intercede supernaturally to continue the war. She simply relies on the nature of Pandaros, who very humanly ignites renewed conflict.

Book Five deals almost exclusively with the brave deeds of Diomedes, and has been called the "Diomedia." Some critics believe that this section of the *Iliad* was composed as a separate story and added to the *Iliad* later. This theory is based on the fact that the chapter does nothing to advance the plot of the conflict between Achilleus and Agamemnon.

However, it is also true that Diomedes presents a strong contrast to Achilleus. While the two men are both strong in battle, favored by the gods, and leaders of men, Diomedes shares none of Achilleus' impetuousness. While Achilleus is back at the ships nursing his grudge against Agamemnon, Diomedes is in the heart of the conflict and fights bravely even after he is badly injured. While Diomedes is never slighted in the same way as Achilleus, there are examples throughout the *Iliad* of disagreements between Diomedes and Agamemnon. In every one of these cases, Diomedes calmly defers to Agamemnon without complaint, even when Agamemnon is not acting wisely. His unfailing tact and courtesy are in sharp contrast to Achilleus' long-held anger.

Study Questions

1. Who decides to break the truce between the Trojans and Achaians?

2. How is the truce broken?

3. Who is the main character portrayed in Book Five?

4. What name has been given to this book?
5. Who appears to Diomedes when he is injured by Pandaros?
6. What two things does Athene give to Diomedes?
7. What instruction goes with these gifts?
8. What is the exception to this rule, and why?
9. How is Diomedes like Achilleus?
10. How is he different?

Answers

1. The gods decide to break the truce at the urging of Hera and Athene.

2. Athene convinces Pandaros to gain glory by shooting Menelaos, which he does.

3. Diomedes is the main character in Book five.

4. This book has been called the "Diomedia."

5. Athene appears to Diomedes when he is injured.

6. Athene gives Diomedes strength for the battle and the ability to distinguish gods from men.

7. Diomedes is instructed never to engage a god in battle.

8. Diomedes is allowed to confront Aphrodite, because she has no place on the battlefield.

9. Like Achilleus, Diomedes is favored by the gods, strong in battle and a leader.

10. Unlike Achilleus, Diomedes is in control of his emotions and defers to his leaders.

Suggested Essay Topics

1. Discuss what Pandaros had to gain by breaking the truce. What elements of the culture lead him to give in to Athene's suggestion?

2. Compare and contrast Diomedes and Achilleus as heroes. Use specific instances from the text to support your claims.

Book Six

New Characters:

Adrestos: *a Trojan fighter who pleads with Menelaos to take him alive rather than kill him*

Helenos: *son of Priam who urges Hektor to gather the Trojan women to beseech Athene*

Glaukos: *Trojan warrior who exchanges a promise of friendship with Diomedes*

Hekabe: *Priam's wife and Hector's mother, who chooses her best robe as a gift to Athene*

Theano: *priestess of Athene who presents the gift with a prayer to the goddess*

Andromache: *Hektor's wife who tries to convince him not to go back to the battle*

Astyanax: *Hektor's infant son*

Summary

Book Six continues on the same day of fighting, and the Achaians have the advantage. Adrestos is captured by Menelaos and pleads for his life, promising ransom. While at first Menelaos has pity, a sharp rebuke from Agamemnon convinces him not to spare the Trojan's life. Nestor urges the Achaians to continue their assault and not stop to gather the spoils.

The Achaians succeed in pushing the Trojans to retreat. Helenos then advises Hektor to return to Troy and gather the women together to beseech Athene for help with Diomedes. Hektor agrees and heads for the city, urging the warriors to keep up the fight while he is gone.

Meanwhile, Diomedes and Glaukos face each other for a duel. However, before beginning any fighting, Diomedes asks Glaukos to identify himself, since he has never seen him before. It soon becomes apparent that the grandfathers of the two men were friends. The men decide to honor this pact of friendship and to refrain from fighting each other. Armor is exchanged as a sign of their bond.

When Hektor reaches Troy he is met by his mother, Hekuba,

and he tells her to gather the women together and make sacrifice to the goddess Athene. He then goes to the house of Alexandros (Paris) and finds him at home in the company of Helen. Hektor angrily points out that the rest of the Trojans are fighting valiantly in a battle that Paris caused while he lulls about at home. Paris tells Hektor that Helen had just convinced him to join the battle and that he was on his way.

Hektor then goes to find his wife. He finds her with his son, Astyanax, watching the battle from the city walls. Andromache pleads with her husband not to return to the battle. She has lost her father and her brothers to Achilleus and does not wish to lose Hektor as well. Hektor, however, is duty-bound to return to the fighting. He admits to feeling that Troy will fall eventually to the Achaians, but cannot shirk his responsibilities. He reminds Andromache that his fate is in the hands of the gods either way, and then leaves to return to battle.

Analysis

In this chapter we have the vivid picture of Adrestos pleading for his life, offering Menelaos great ransom. This is one of several examples throughout the *Iliad* of captured warriors grabbing the knees of their captor in a desperate gesture of supplication. In this case, Menelaos is moved by the display, and is ready to let Adrestos live. Agamemnon, however, feels no such pity. He reproves Menelaos for letting the man manipulate his feelings. Then he ruthlessly kills Adrestos himself. In every other instance of this pleading, the end will be the same. Mercy is not applauded by the Achaians. Perhaps this is one reason why Agamemnon is considered such a mighty warrior, while Menelaos is seen as his inferior in battle. Great warriors in this culture must be ruthless and unfeeling.

As Diomedes and Glaukos meet each other in battle, they pause to determine each other's background. The *Iliad* is full of similar, long accounts of ancestry and family achievements. An individual's identity is strongly tied to his heritage. When these two warriors discover a friendship between their grandparents, they immediately make a pact of friendship. It is clear from this behavior that bonds of friendship supersede all other obligations—even when the bond was made two generations earlier. This incident is in sharp contrast to the barbaric behavior of the battle all around them. While Diomedes can, and is obligated to, slaughter any and all other Trojans, he will not harm Glaukos. The bond of friendship is a central tenet of the heroic code, and its influence is seen several times throughout the epic.

In this book we find Paris again shirking his duties. He lounges at home with Helen, surrounded by the women of his household while the battle continues without him. When Hektor once again gives him an angry lecture about responsibility, Paris responds that he was on his way back to the battle. Nothing about Paris' behavior supports this claim. Most likely he was just being cowardly and letting the other Trojans fight his battle for him. Paris' actions are particularly irksome to Hektor, who takes his responsibility very seriously.

At the end of this book, Hektor admits to Andromache that he is fairly certain the Trojans will be defeated in the end. Yet even

facing near-certain defeat, Hektor does not try to escape his responsibilities. He has a duty as commander of the forces to fight to
the end. Hektor has a strong belief in fate and knows that the will
of the gods will be done regardless of the behavior of mortals. While
he fears for his wife and son after the fall of Troy, he must accept
fate and uphold his duties.

Hektor's strong ties to family and their obvious importance to
him have led some critics to argue that he symbolizes family values and unity. Hektor's wife and son are prominent in the *Iliad*, as
are his parents. He often thinks of them, and he fears for their safety.
He is aware that if Troy is taken, his wife will be given to an Achaian
as a war prize and his son will most likely be killed. Andromache
here represents the innocence of everyday life. Her exchange with
Hektor underlines the loss caused to those who remain behind
when any warrior is killed. The prominence of Hektor's family in
the epic is in sharp contrast to the Achaian heroes who rarely speak
of home and family. This is partly due to the fact that the Achaian
homeland is far away; thus, the Achaians cannot be a part of the
action on the home front. However, there is a difference in Hektor's
attitude and a softer quality to his leadership. Though fearful and
brave in battle, he lives for more than glory in war. This will become clearer as the epic progresses.

Study Questions

1. Does Menelaos wish to kill Adrestos?

2. What ends up happening to Adrestos?

3. What is Nestor's advice to the Achaians?

4. Why does Hektor return to the city?

5. What do Diomedes and Glaukos discover about each other
   as they introduce themselves?

6. What do they do after making this discovery?

7. What do they do to symbolize this?

8. Where does Hektor find Paris, and how does he react?

9. Why does Andromache plead with Hektor not to return to
   battle?

10. Does Hektor believe the Trojans will defeat the Achaians?

Answers

1. Menelaos has pity on Adrestos and does not wish to kill him.

2. Adrestos is killed coldly by Agamemnon.

3. Nestor advises the Achaians to attack the Trojans without stopping to take the spoils.

4. Hektor returns to the city to gather the women together to sacrifice to Athene.

5. They discover that there was a bond of friendship between their grandparents.

6. They make a pact not to harm one another in battle.

7. Armor is exchanged to symbolize the bond of friendship.

8. Hektor finds Paris at home with the women of his household. He gives Paris a lecture about his failure to face his responsibilities.

9. Andromache has lost her father and brothers already in the battle, and does not wish to lose her husband as well. She also fears for their young son Astyanax.

10. Hektor knows in his heart that the Trojans will be defeated.

Suggested Essay Topics

1. Compare Hektor's attitude and behavior to that of Paris, especially their desires for the fate of Troy and looming destruction.

2. Discuss the ways in which Hektor serves as a symbol for the value of home and family in the epic and how this contrasts with the approach of Agamemnon.

Book Seven

New Characters:

Talthybios: *Achaian herald who breaks up the duel*

Poseidon: *also called "Earthshaker"; the god of the sea*

Summary

The Trojans are greatly encouraged as Hektor and Paris rush back to the battlefield. Athene is distressed at the destruction these two cause and she meets with Apollo. Together they decide to encourage Hektor to challenge an Achaian to a duel. This plan will give the rest of the warriors a reprieve from the fighting. They put the idea in Helenos' head, and he brings the suggestion to Hektor.

Hektor holds back the Trojans, and they all sit down on the battlefield. Likewise, Agamemnon holds back the Achaians, and they all sit on the battlefield to hear what Hektor has to say. Hektor offers his challenge, and Menelaos is the first to accept the task. However, he is dissuaded from fighting by the Achaians who know that Hektor is a far superior warrior. Nestor then urges the Achaians to act like men and to accept the challenge. After his speech, nine of the Achaians rise to volunteer. When lots are cast to choose among them, Telamonian Aias is chosen.

Prayers are offered to Zeus and the duel begins. The men are fairly evenly matched, and the fighting is fierce. When the sky darkens, a herald from each side holds his stave between the two and separates them. Gifts are exchanged, and both men return to their armies.

Agamemnon calls the Achaian leaders together for a strategy meeting and a great feast is prepared. Nestor suggests that a truce should be called to allow the Achaians to properly bury their dead. He also suggests that the Achaians build a high, towered wall around their camp to keep back the Trojans. Meanwhile, the Trojans also hold counsel and Antenor advises them to give up Helen in order to avoid great disaster. Paris is willing to give up the treasure taken and to add greater treasure, but he refuses to relinquish Helen. Priam then suggests that a truce be called so that the Trojans can bury their dead.

Idaios is sent the next morning to the Achaian camp to convey the Trojan message. While the Achaians quickly reject the offer of treasure from Paris, both sides nonetheless agree to a truce to bury the dead. Both armies tend to their dead, burning the bodies on great funeral pyres. Then the Achaians build their wall and surround it with a deep ditch full of stakes. As the gods watch from Olympus, Poseidon angrily points out that the Achaians neglected to offer gifts to the gods before building their wall. To placate him, Zeus agrees to sweep the wall into the sea after the Achaians have left Troy. Both the Trojans and Achaians feast and then sleep.

Analysis

Here we see the gods intervening in the battle to give both sides some much needed rest. Throughout the story, the gods are constantly involving themselves at every level to control the outcome of the fighting. In this case, they do not appear in disguise, but instead put the idea for what they desire in the mind of a mortal. They are confident enough that the men will agree to the plan that they do not need to appear in physical form. Again, there has been no supernatural event, only a gentle urging to convince men to act.

Hektor's strength as a warrior is highlighted in this book when no Achaian rushes to accept his challenge to a duel. When

Menelaos volunteers, his companions will not allow him to fight, as Hektor is a far greater warrior. It takes another stirring speech by Nestor to stir the best Achaian warriors to step forward. Nestor represents the wisdom of age. He has been a witness to an epoch of great strength and superior people. With his stories of past glory, he attempts to prod the Achaians to greater courage and strength in battle. All through the *Iliad*, Nestor will continually offer roughly the same motivational speech, playing on the Achaian fear of being labeled a coward. While this seems to be a powerful motivator, the Achaians constantly need to be reminded. This is not surprising when you consider the fact that a duel of this sort would normally end with the death of one of the parties.

Both armies desire a truce at this point during which to bury their dead. Proper burial is a central issue of this culture and a major theme of the *Iliad*. Later in the epic there is a striking example of a hero's burial in the funeral rites for Patroklos. The men who have died thus far did not hold the same status, and their burial will be far less elaborate. However, it is very important that their bodies be properly treated, and not left to decay. A recurring phrase is "left for the dogs"; or left for animals to devour and therefore defile. This is the ultimate insult to a warrior, and many times the phrase is used as a threat against an opponent in battle. A dead man's soul cannot peacefully enter the afterlife until proper burial steps have been taken. Many battles described in the *Iliad* will occur over the bodies of those who have been killed. While the warrior's companions wish to bring the body back and properly bury it, the opposing warriors seek to strip it of valuable armor and then mistreat it as a symbol of their power and victory.

This chapter also describes the building of the Achaian wall. This is an important tactical move on their part. The wall and its surrounding ditch will protect the Achaians to some degree from Trojan assault. The Achaian wall also serves as a parallel to the Trojan wall. The Trojans built the great wall around their city with the help and blessing of Poseidon. They failed, however, to compensate the god for his trouble. Poseidon's siding with the Achaians in the battle is a direct result of that breach. The Achaian wall is built without the help of the gods, and without sacrifice to them. For this reason, the gods are angered by its presence and Zeus promises that after the Achaians sail home the wall will be destroyed.

Study Questions

1. Whose idea is it to call a truce and have Hektor challenge an Achaian to a duel, and why?

2. Who first accepts Hektor's challenge?

3. Does he fight Hektor? Why?

4. Who volunteers next and why?

5. How is the man to fight Hektor finally chosen, and who is it?

6. Who is the stronger fighter in the duel?

7. How does the duel end?

8. What do both sides request after counsel that evening?

9. Why is it important to the warriors to bury their dead?

10. What do the Achaians do during the truce?

Answers

1. Athene and Apollo decide to have Hektor offer a duel in order to give the other warriors a break from the fighting.

2. While no one at first volunteers to fight Hektor, Menelaos finally comes forward.

3. Menelaos does not fight Hektor because his companions know he is not strong enough to stand up to the Trojan.

4. Nine of the best Achaians step forward after an inspiring speech by Nestor.

5. Aias is chosen by casting lots.

6. Hektor and Aias are equally matched in the duel and neither has the advantage.

7. The duel ends when it grows dark and a herald from each side parts the fighters.

8. Both sides request a truce to bury their dead.

9. The warriors wish to bury the dead so that their souls will be allowed peaceful entry into the Underworld and so that the bodies will not be defiled on the field.

10. During the truce, the Achaians burn their dead, hold a funeral feast, and build a great wall surrounded by a ditch to hold back the Trojans.

Suggested Essay Topics

1. Compare the speeches that Nestor offers to the Achaians. What is similar among them about the language he uses? How are they different? What effect do they have on the warriors? How would you define Nestor's role?

2. Discuss the different ways the gods intervene in the *Iliad* to shape the actions of mortals. In what form do they appear? Are they recognized? Is their advice always taken?

Book Eight

New Character:

Teukros: *Achaian warrior who kills many Trojans*

Summary

Book Eight opens with a fierce warning from Zeus. He promises dire consequences to any immortal who attempts to help either the Trojans or the Achaians. Athene asks permission to give advice to the Achaians without actually aiding them in battle, and Zeus agrees. Zeus then leaves for Mount Ida, where he will have a clear view of the battlefield and will be left in peace to survey the action.

Meanwhile, both armies prepare for battle, and the fighting begins again in earnest. At noon, Zeus takes out his golden scales and weighs the fates of the Trojans and the Achaians. The fate of the Achaians sinks, while the Trojan's fate is lifted high. Shortly after this, the Achaians lose courage, and fare badly in the fighting. They turn and run to the ships, and many are pinned in the space between the Trojans and the wall.

Hera then tries to convince Poseidon to aid the Achaians. Poseidon is afraid of the consequences of disobeying Zeus, though, and he refuses. Agamemnon, however, prays to Zeus, who pities the Achaians, not wanting them to be completely destroyed. Zeus sends an omen: an eagle with a fawn in its talons that is dropped next to the Achaian altar to Zeus. This sign rallies the Achaians for a time, but they are soon pushed back again to the ditch, and then back to the ships.

Hera and Athene are dismayed by the dire situation for the Achaians, and they harness a team of horses to take them into the battle. Zeus is furious when he sees what they have done, and is-

sues a severe threat to them if they choose to intervene on behalf of the Achaians. The two goddesses agree to let fate run its course, and they turn back.

The fighting ends with nightfall, and the Trojans camp on the plain by the Achaian wall. Hektor orders the Trojans not to allow the Achaians to escape in their ships during the night. Food is brought from the city, and the Trojans build their fires and wait for dawn to resume the fighting.

Analysis

This book opens with an example of the conflict between Zeus and the other immortals over the fate of the war. While the immortals are eager to lend their substantial strength to their favorite side, Zeus is continually warning them not to interfere. Here again, Zeus indicates that he favors bringing an end to the war, and strongly threatens the other gods to keep their distance. So forceful are his words that the assembly is shocked to hear them. Still, Athene is bold enough to request permission to give advice to the Achaians. Zeus surprisingly agrees. The impression we get from this behavior is of a stern parent reprimanding a group of unruly children. While the parent has ultimate control, he does not have control over every little action carried out by one of his charges. The children are constantly getting into trouble by not listening. Unsurprisingly, before the book is over, Hera and Athene are caught trying to enter the battle on behalf of the Achaians.

Another view of the immortals in this chapter involves the scales of fate. The scales are seen several times during the course of the narrative, and each time they show who will emerge victorious in the situation at hand. This time the scales weigh the outcome of the day's fighting, and it is clear that the Trojans will hold the advantage. Shortly after, the battle on the field mirrors the outcome of the scales, and the Achaians are forced back to their ships. The scales of fate show that Zeus is not exactly in charge of the events happening on earth. Rather, he himself is bound by the limits of fate, and his actions merely serve to bring about fate's predetermined outcome. The scales never represent supernatural intervention in the lives of man; instead, they reveal what must happen due to the nature of things.

Study Questions

1. Why does Zeus warn the gods to stay out of the conflict?

2. Where does Zeus go to watch the battle?

3. What sign are we given that the Trojans will come out ahead in this day's fighting?

4. Who does Hera ask to help her intervene for the Achaians?

5. What is his answer?

6. What omen does Zeus send to Agamemnon to let him know all will be well?

7. Which two goddesses attempt to ride into the battle to help

the Achaians?

8. Are they successful?

9. Where are the two armies at the close of this day's fighting?

10. Why does Hektor choose to camp where he does?

Answers

1. Zeus wishes to bring the war to a quick end and does not want the gods to interfere.

2. Zeus watches the battle from Mount Ida.

3. Zeus holds up the scales of fate and the Achaians' side sinks down.

4. Hera tries to enlist the help of Poseidon.

5. Poseidon refuses to get involved, knowing that his brother Zeus is more powerful.

6. An eagle drops a fawn next to the Achaian altar to Zeus.

7. Hera and Athene harness their horses to ride into the battle to help the Achaians.

8. Zeus discovers their plan, and they are forced to return to Olympus.

9. The Achaians have been forced back behind their wall, and the Trojans are camped right up against its other side.

10. Hektor camps by the wall to ensure that the Achaians do not try to escape in the night with their ships, and also to maintain an advantage for the next day's fighting.

Suggested Essay Topics

1. Explore the many images of birds in the *Iliad* and their significance to the narrative. How much faith do the Trojans and Achaians have in omens?

2. How much control does Zeus have over the immortals? How much control does he have over the actions of mortals? What is the relationship of fate to the gods?

Book Nine

New Character:

Phoinix: *old friend and teacher of Achilleus, sent to him with Agamemnon's peace offer*

Summary

As Book Nine opens, the Achaians are in a panic. Agamemnon calls an assembly and tearfully suggests fleeing in their ships. It is Diomedes who finally protests against this plan, chastising Agamemnon for cowardice. He succeeds in rallying the Achaians to go on with the fight. Nestor then stands and suggests that a guard be set up outside the wall to protect against a surprise attack, and that a feast be held for the elders as they decide their plan of action.

As the elders feast, Nestor points out that the present difficulty is a direct result of Agamemnon's feud with Achilleus. He suggests returning Briseis and making peace with Achilleus so that he will return to fight with the Achaians. Agamemnon is now ready to

admit fault, and he agrees to return Briseis to Achilleus, along with a sworn oath that he has not touched her and a generous array of gifts. Phoinix, Aias, and Odysseus, all friends of Achilleus, are sent to give him the message.

Achilleus warmly receives his friends into his hut, but he is still too angry to accept Agamemnon's peace offering, explaining that even 10 or 20 times the amount of treasure offered could not repay the wrong done to him. In the morning he plans to sail for home, and he advises his friends to do the same. Phoinix makes an emotional appeal to Achilleus to change his mind and forgive, but to no avail. Odysseus and Aias are sent to take the message back to Agamemnon, while Phoinix remains with Achilleus.

Achilleus' answer shocks Agamemnon. Diomedes then declares that it was a mistake to have tried to entreat such a proud man with offers of great treasure. He advises them to get some sleep and in the morning do the best they can to defend their ships.

Analysis

At this point, Agamemnon sees only disastrous consequences in the fighting to come. He is so frightened he completely loses sight of the omens he has been given as proof of eventual Achaian victory and he advocates running away. He reveals himself in this book as lacking the substance and character necessary to be a great leader. He is completely dependent on his advisors to make important tactical decisions. It is Diomedes who reminds him of his dignity and duties as commander of the forces. Diomedes shows his mettle by announcing that even if everyone else runs away, he will stay and fight to the end, believing that Troy will eventually fall.

Nestor very diplomatically points a finger at Agamemnon, making it clear that he is at fault for much of the Achaian situation. Had Agamemnon not quarreled with Achilleus, they would surely be in a better strategic position. It is very precarious to find fault with such a great leader, but Nestor is not afraid to speak the truth. Nestor again represents the voice of reason and good sense, and Agamemnon agrees.

Achilleus, on the other hand, is not being at all reasonable. It is not enough for him that Agamemnon has admitted his error and requested his return to the battle. It is clear from this passage that

Achilleus is not interested in material things. He will not give up until Agamemnon is brought to his knees. While both men were acting childish, it originally seemed that most of the blame rested with Agamemnon. However, in refusing an honest apology and offer of recompense, Achilleus now appears morally inferior. The oddity of Achilleus' refusal is highlighted in the stunned reaction of the Achaians when they hear the news. His tragic flaw becomes vividly apparent here as his pride stands in the way of his intellect. This incident is a turning point in the narrative, and for some time afterward, things will go very badly for the Achaians.

Study Questions

1. What plan does Agamemnon suggest as the book opens?
2. Who dissuades him and why?
3. What is Nestor's advice to Agamemnon?
4. What does Agamemnon offer to give Achilleus?
5. Who is sent to bring the message to Achilleus?
6. How are the messengers received?
7. Does Achilleus accept Agamemnon's offer?
8. Why does Achilleus act as he does?
9. What is the Achaian reaction to Achilleus' answer?
10. What is Diomedes' response?

Answers

1. Agamemnon suggests that the Achaians escape in their ships and sail home.
2. Diomedes dissuades him, because he trusts that Troy will fall. He also thinks it is too dangerous for the Achaians to flee by sea.
3. Nestor advises Agamemnon to make peace with Achilleus.
4. Agamemnon agrees to return Briseis, along with an oath that he has not touched her, as well as many valuable gifts.
5. Odysseus, Aias, and Phoinix are sent to Achilleus.

6. Achilleus receives the messengers warmly.

7. Achilleus refuses Agamemnon's offer of reconciliation.

8. Achilleus lets his pride stand in the way of reason. He wants Agamemnon to be completely humbled in front of him before he will consent to fight again with the Achaians.

9. The Achaians are shocked that Achilleus would refuse such a generous offer.

10. Diomedes angrily suggests that it was a mistake to make such a generous offer to such a foolish man.

Suggested Essay Topics

1. Agamemnon and Achilleus have been involved in their quarrel now since the beginning of the *Iliad*. Compare and contrast each man's response to the situation as events unfold.

2. How is Diomedes' character defined in this chapter? How does he function as a foil to Achilleus?

Book Ten

New Characters:

Dolon: *Trojan warrior who agrees to spy on the Achaians in return for treasure*

Rhesos: *King of the Thracians, killed on a spy mission by Diomedes*

Summary

The seriousness of the Achaian situation keeps Agamemnon from sleeping. He rises and gathers the leaders of the Achaian forces together to discuss strategy. They decide to send spies into the Trojan camps to see what they can learn of the Trojan battle plans. Diomedes offers to go if he can bring a companion for security. Odysseus is chosen and they go, fully armed.

On the way, they encounter Dolon, a Trojan soldier sent out to spy on the Achaians. After initially letting him pass, they chase him down and capture him. Dolon is terrified and quickly confesses his mission. He also reveals the location of Hektor, the type of guards set up by the Trojans, the positions of various fighting units, and the sleeping area of a newly arrived and unprotected force from Thrace. As Dolan attempts to plead for mercy, Diomedes kills him with his sword and takes his clothes and weapon. These spoils are offered as gifts to Athene.

Diomedes and Odysseus then head for the Thracian camp and kill 12 sleeping Thracians. The thirteenth man killed is the Thracian king, Rhesos, owner of a splendid team of horses. The Achaians then release the horses and escape with them, heading back to their ships. When they return with their spoils, they are joyfully received by the Achaians. The two men wash themselves in the sea, sit down to a meal, and make offerings to Athene.

Analysis

Diomedes again shows his loyalty to the Achaian cause by being the first to volunteer to infiltrate the Trojan camps. Knowledge of troop configuration and security plans would be a real advantage to the Achaians, who are in a very vulnerable position. Realizing the danger of the mission, Diomedes goes only on the condition that he can choose a companion for security. Diomedes has consistently been among the first to volunteer for any challenge presented. This, again, is in sharp contrast to Achilleus, who lets his differences with Agamemnon keep him completely removed from battle, where he is sorely needed.

In this book we see another example of a Trojan warrior pleading for his life. When Diomedes and Odysseus capture Dolon, the trembling Trojan tries to convince them to take him alive. While Diomedes has volunteered to spy out of a sense of duty and responsibility, Dolon has offered for selfish reasons. Hektor has promised him that Achilleus' horses would be his as reward. Having no loyalty to the Trojan cause, he does not hesitate to reveal every tactical secret he knows when he runs into danger. Like every other Trojan who pleads for mercy, Dolon has no chance. As soon as he has given Diomedes the information, he is killed with a sword and his armor is taken as spoils.

The murder of the sleeping troops from Thrace seems particularly savage. These men are not even given a chance to defend themselves. However, the slain were part of a contingent of fresh troops. As such, they would be particularly dangerous to the Achaians, who are by now rather battle-weary. The horses taken are quite a magnificent prize, and have the added benefit of offering a means of quick escape for Odysseus and Diomedes.

Study Questions

1. Who is the first to volunteer for the spy mission into the Trojan camp?
2. Who does he choose to go with him, and why?
3. What do the Achaians hope to gain by the mission?
4. Who is sent on a similar mission for the Trojans?
5. What are his motivations?
6. Who catches whom spying?
7. What do they learn?
8. Which unit of Trojan fighters are Diomedes and Odysseus most interested in?
9. What becomes of Dolon?
10. Who is later killed and what is taken?

Answers

1. Diomedes is the first to volunteer to spy on the Trojans.
2. Diomedes chooses Odysseus for his strength and fighting ability.
3. The Achaians hope to learn where various groups of Trojans will attack and where they are vulnerable.
4. Dolon is sent by the Trojans to spy on the Achaian camp.
5. Dolon volunteers only when he is promised Achilleus' horses as reward.
6. Diomedes and Odysseus catch Dolon and realize he is going to spy on the Achaians.
7. Dolon reveals everything he knows, including Hektor's

whereabouts, the position of several other key Trojan units, and the security measures taken by the Trojans.

8. Diomedes and Odysseus are most interested in a fresh unit that has arrived from Thrace.

9. He pleads for his life, but is killed by Diomedes.

10. Diomedes and Odysseus kill 12 Thracian warriors and their king, Rhesos. They take a team of remarkable horses and use them to escape back to their camp.

Suggested Essay Topics

1. Compare and contrast Dolon and Diomedes. Both men are spies for their armies. What are their motives? How do these motives affect their actions?

2. Agamemnon is distressed at the number of Trojan fires burning outside the Achaian wall. Explore the symbol of fire here and elsewhere in the *Iliad*. What are fire's immediate dangers? What do these fires foreshadow?

Book Eleven

New Characters:

Machaon: *wounded Achaian carried out of battle by Nestor*

Eurypylos: *wounded Achaian who asks Patroklos to tend his wound*

Summary

As dawn breaks, the Achaians and Trojans arm for battle. Both sides fight fiercely, and the Achaians successfully break the Trojan line, forcing the enemy all the way back to the city walls. Then, however, the Trojans rally and soon Agamemnon is hit in the arm with a spear. He fights for a while, but eventually gives in to his wound and leaves the field. Shortly thereafter, Antenor shoots Diomedes through the foot with an arrow and he too is out of the battle. Then Odysseus is stabbed through his shield, and he also retreats to the camp. Aias continues fighting bravely, holding back the Trojans almost single-handedly.

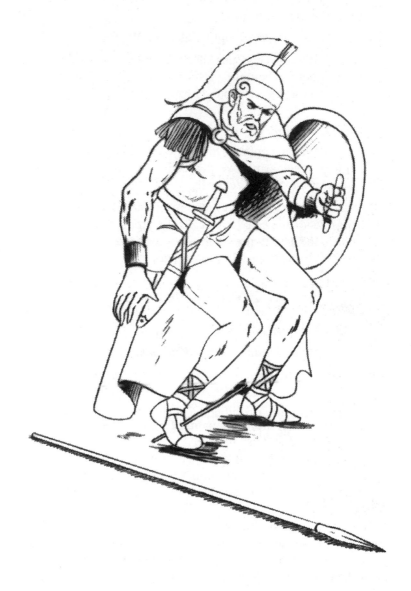

Meanwhile, Achilleus watches the action from the stern of his ship. He senses that the Achaians now sorely need him, and that they will be brought to their knees to beg him to return to the battle. When he sees Nestor taking a wounded man from the battle, he sends Patroklos to him for news. Patroklos reaches Nestor and is informed of the day's events. Nestor begs Patroklos to use his influence on Achilleus to convince him to bring his fresh troops into the battle. He also suggests that if Achilleus will not go, he could send Patroklos with the Myrmidon army. Nestor points out that if Patroklos wears Achilleus' great armor, the Trojans may mistake him for Achilleus and retreat to the city.

Patroklos is moved by Nestor's speech and sets off to return to Achilleus. On the way he is met by Eurypylos, wounded in the thigh by an arrow. Eurypylos gives a grim account of the Achaian position and requests that Patroklos help him with his wound. Patroklos cannot refuse, and stops to tend the wound.

Analysis

In very short succession, each of the strongest Achaian fighters is wounded and unable to fight. It has been argued that these events are a direct result of Achilleus' stubborn refusal to set aside his pride and accept Agamemnon's generous offer of reconciliation. With or without these injuries, Achilleus and his troops are sorely missed. Watching the action from the safety of his ship, Achilleus does not decide to rush in and help his fellow warriors defend themselves. Instead, he distastefully revels in the Achaian's distress. In his pride, he believes that this rout will lead them to come begging on their knees for his return.

Rather than show his interest in the events of the battle, Achilleus sends Patroklos to obtain information. Patroklos is Achilleus closest friend and companion, and he represents the human side of Achilleus. While Achilleus broods, Patroklos acts on his concern for the Achaians by approaching Nestor. Patroklos hears the dire news of the battle from Nestor, after which the wise old warrior offers yet another of his encouraging speeches. His goal is to convince Patroklos to use his influence with Achilleus to have him change his mind and enter the battle. He also offers an alternate plan. If Achilleus will not relent and go to war himself, per-

haps he can send Patroklos dressed in his armor. The mere sight of the great armor may turn the tables for the Achaians. The importance of this plan is that Nestor is offering Achilleus a way to help his fellow Achaians without losing face. Nestor wisely realizes that Achilleus is held back only by his pride, and that he actually has great affection for the Achaian warriors.

Patroklos is prevented from returning immediately to Achilleus by Eurypylos. Even though Patroklos has urgent news to bring to his companion, he cannot ignore the plight of the wounded Eurypylos, who requests his aid. This episode dramatically underscores the generous and caring nature of Patroklos. Such behavior is in stark contrast to that of Achilleus, who sits on the sidelines watching the Achaians fall, knowing all the while that his help could save many lives.

Study Questions

1. Which of the great Achaian fighters are wounded in this chapter?

2. Who is the only great fighter left fighting?

3. Where is Achilleus as he watches the action?

4. What is Achilleus' attitude toward the events taking place?

5. What prompts Achilleus to desire news of the battle?

6. How does Achilleus decide to obtain this information?

7. What does Nestor ask Patroklos to do?

8. What is Nestor's alternate plan?

9. Why does he think this alternate plan will work?

10. What stops Patroklos from returning directly to Achilleus?

Answers

1. Agamemnon, Diomedes, and Odysseus are all wounded in rapid succession.

2. Aias is the only great fighter left on the field.

3. Achilleus watches from the safety of the stern of his ship.

4. Achilleus believes that with so many great men injured, the Achaians are sure to come to him begging his forgiveness.

5. Achilleus sees Nestor leading a wounded man from the field.

6. Achilleus decides to send Patroklos to Nestor to learn news of the battle.

7. Nestor asks Patroklos to convince Achilleus to give up his grudge and fight.

8. If Achilleus will not fight, Nestor suggests that he send Patroklos to the field in Achilleus' armor.

9. Nestor believes that the Trojans are so impressed with the

strength of Achilleus that the mere sight of his armor in battle will be enough to send them into retreat.

10.   Patroklos is prevented from returning immediately to Achilleus by Eurypylos, who has been badly wounded and requests help from Patroklos in tending to the wound.

Suggested Essay Topics

1.   Compare the nature and temperament of Patroklos to that of his companion, Achilleus. How does each man react to the Achaian difficulty in battle? What is each man's reaction to advice?

2.   Discuss how Achilleus has become unable to act due to his pride.

Books Twelve and Thirteen

New Characters:

Poulydamas: *Trojan soldier who advises Hektor to leave horses and attack the wall on foot*

Meriones: *Achaian warrior who comes to Idomeneus to replace his broken spear*

Summary

The Achaians are penned back by their ships and Hektor attempts to bring his army over the ditch in front of the wall. However, as the Trojan horses are afraid of the ditch, crossing with the chariots is deemed too difficult. The Trojans decide to leave their horses and attempt to break through the wall on foot.

As Hektor, Poulydamas, and their men prepare to cross the ditch, they see an omen. An eagle holding a live snake flies over, and the snake twists and bites its captor in the neck. The eagle cries out and drops the snake among the men, who are gripped with fright at such a strong sign from Zeus. Poulydamas advises Hektor to heed the warning and turn back. However, Hektor is determined to attack and leads the charge on the wall. The two armies fight

bitterly at the wall and many men on both sides are killed. Finally, Hektor hurls a great rock at the doors of the double gates and smashes the hinges, shattering the doors. The Trojans stream inside, sending the Achaians running for their ships in panic.

Poseidon, watching the Achaians fighting to save their ships, feels pity for them and great anger at Zeus. He mounts his chariot and rides over the sea to the battle. He leaves his horses and moves among the Achaians in the guise of Kalchas, the seer, giving the warriors new strength and courage for battle. The battle rages on, and Idomeneus fights bravely, bringing down many Trojans.

Analysis

Homer is not one for excessive suspense. In the first paragraph of Book Twelve, he indicates that Troy is sacked in the tenth year and all the leading Trojan men are killed. While the outcome of the war had previously been more subtly alluded to, this statement is particularly blunt. We are reminded that the audience would have

known the ultimate outcome of the war anyway. The purpose of
the *Iliad* is not to relate the overall story of the Trojan War, but to
tell of the quarrel between Achilleus and Agamemnon, and its disastrous effects.

The events related here highlight the difficulty of reading the
omens. We are told that Zeus is determined to give the victory to
Hektor, yet the signs would suggest otherwise. What Hektor fails
to see is the limit of Zeus' plan. Zeus promises victory only up to
the ships of the Achaians. While Hektor interprets this to mean
ultimate victory, the reality is the Achaians will come back strongly
after the Trojans reach the Achaian ships. When an eagle suddenly
drops a writhing serpent in the midst of the Trojan forces,
Poulydamas understandably takes it to be a rather negative omen.
Hektor disregards his pessimism and charges ahead. Hektor is incredibly successful, pushing right through the Achaian wall and
forcing the terrified Achaians all the way back to the ships. However, Poulydamas has read the omen correctly as a sign of the ultimate destruction of Troy. Regardless of omens, Hektor's
responsibility will not allow him to run from conflict.

The gods are still at odds with Zeus over his plan to help
Achilleus by giving glory to Hektor. Poseidon believes the slaughter of the Achaians is unfair, and once again defies Zeus by rushing
in to help them defend themselves. While Zeus and Poseidon are
brothers, Poseidon knows that Zeus is older and wiser, and has the
upper hand. He therefore wisely avoids helping the Achaians
openly. Instead, he stays quietly in the background out of Zeus'
sight, strengthening and encouraging the warriors.

Hektor gives Paris another lecture about his lack of bravery.
This time, however, it appears that Paris has been fighting after all.
Even in battle, though, Paris tends to keep away from the fiercest
segments of the fighting. His lack of responsibility is a constant
bane to Hektor, who serves as the symbol of duty and control.
Homer has made it plain elsewhere that Hektor is aware that Troy
will fall. Even so, he will fight to the end, doing what he can to save
his loved ones behind the wall. While Paris is not willing to give
Helen back to Menelaos, his exploits on the battlefield show a real
lack of concern for the safety of those left in Troy.

Study Questions

1. What information do we learn in Book Twelve about the war's outcome?

2. What initial difficulty do the Trojans face in storming the Achaian wall?

3. What do they decide to do about it?

4. What omen do the Trojan's see as they prepare to assault the wall?

5. How does Poulydamas interpret the sign, and what is his advice to Hektor?

6. What does Hektor decide to do?

7. Are the Trojans successful in breaking through the wall?

8. Which god comes to the aid of the Achaians?

9. How does he avoid being noticed by Zeus?

10. Why doesn't he stand up to Zeus?

Answers

1. In the first paragraph of Book Twelve, we learn that the Trojans will be defeated in the tenth year of the war, and that all the leading Trojan men will be killed.

2. The Trojan horses are afraid of the ditch, and the ditch is too wide for them to jump.

3. The Trojans decide to leave their horses and attack the wall on foot.

4. An eagle holding a live snake flies over the Trojans, is bitten by the snake, and drops it at the feet of the terrified warriors.

5. Poulydamas reads the sign as a warning of what will become of the Trojans and advises Hektor to retreat.

6. Hektor decides to ignore the sign and storm the wall.

7. The Trojans break through the wall when Hektor smashes the gates with a stone.

8. Poseidon pities the Achaians and comes to their aid.

9. Poseidon avoids detection by assuming a disguise and not fighting openly.

10. Though Poseidon is Zeus' brother, he realizes that Zeus has more power and he fears his wrath.

Suggested Essay Topics

1. Discuss the meaning of the omens in Books 12 and 13. What effect do they have on the decisions made on the field? How are they similar to other omens in the *Iliad*?

2. Describe the role of Poulydamas in the epic. Who among the Achaians plays a similar role? How are they treated by their respective leaders?

Books Fourteen and Fifteen

New Character:

Thoas: *advises the Achaians to retreat to their ships*

Summary

Nestor leaves his hut to observe the battle and sees that the Trojans have broken through the Achaian wall. He soon encounters Diomedes, Odysseus, and Agamemnon, and they discuss strategy. Agamemnon proposes that they drag the ships into the sea and sail away under cover of darkness. He sees no point in fighting the Trojans when the gods are on their side. Odysseus chides him for his lack of courage. He points out that if the Achaians know they will retreat in their ships, they will lose the spirit for fighting and be destroyed on the battlefield before they reach the shore. Diomedes then proposes that the three wounded leaders go back to the fighting to encourage the men, and they all agree to do so.

Hera looks down from Olympus and happily sees Poseidon on the battlefield spurring on the Achaians. She immediately thinks of a plan to keep Zeus out of his way. She bathes and perfumes herself, dresses herself in beautiful clothing, and borrows the magic Band of Love and Desire from Aphrodite. She then enlists the aid of Sleep, promising him one of the Graces in marriage if he will

put Zeus to sleep after she has lain with him. She goes to Zeus on Mount Ida, and he is overwhelmed with desire for her, wraps them in clouds and lies with her. Sleep then overtakes him.

Aias and Hektor meet in combat, and Hektor is brought down with a large stone. As he is carried from the battlefield, the Achaians are spurred on and force the Trojans back. As Book Fifteen opens, the Trojans are pushed back across the ditch on the far side of the wall. When Zeus awakens and sees the Trojans in retreat and Hektor lying wounded on the field, he is furious with both Hera and Poseidon. Zeus then lays out the major events that will take place in the battle. Iris is sent to order Poseidon to leave the battle, and Apollo is sent to panic the Achaians, spur on the Trojans, and strengthen Hektor.

When the Achaian army sees Hektor back in the fighting, they are afraid and retreat back to their ships. The Trojans press forward through the wall and the panicked Achaians pray to the gods for their lives. The fighting now takes place among the Achaian ships, and Hektor calls for fire to burn them.

Analysis

Agamemnon is ready to give up and sail for home. He interprets the signs as an indication that the gods now favor Troy, and no longer believes that the Achaians will eventually be victorious. Agamemnon is again showing his weakness and inability to lead. This time it is Odysseus who harshly reminds Agamemnon of his position of responsibility. Odysseus is not quite as diplomatic as Diomedes when facing Agamemnon. He calls Agamemnon a "catastrophe," and reminds him that if they flee, all the fighting of the last nine years would be in vain. Also, it is a tactically dangerous proposition. Many men would certainly be lost in attempting to escape. Agamemnon is in such a state of panic that he is not offended by Odysseus' tone in the least. Diomedes again emerges as the voice of reason, and the men set off to encourage the warriors.

Hera's seduction of Zeus is an interesting picture of the behavior of the gods. Far from being above the desires and temptations of men, Zeus is tricked by the very human element of sexual desire. Though supremely powerful among the gods, Zeus is not capable of perceiving Hera's lie. Likewise, Sleep himself is motivated

by his desire for a woman. While frightened of Zeus' retribution, Sleep quickly agrees to defy him when offered the object of his desire. With Zeus safely asleep, Hera is able to give Poseidon time to openly help the Achaians without fear of discovery.

In Book Fifteen the narrator again reveals the plot. This time Zeus reveals events that will take place in the full scope of the *Iliad*. These include one last drive by the Trojans that will force the Achaians to their ships; the appearance of Patroklos on the battlefield; the death of Sarpedon, Zeus' son, at the hand of Patroklos; the death of Patroklos at the hand of Hektor; and Hektor's death at the hand of Achilleus. At this point the Achaians are certain they will die. They are now fighting for their lives as the Trojans attempt to torch the ships. Zeus delivers his list of coming events to avoid further interference by the gods in his plan to honor Thetis' request to help Achilleus. He reassures them that although things appear grim for the Achaians, they will eventually be victorious.

Study Questions

1. What is Agamemnon's plan of action at the beginning of Book Fourteen?

2. Who dissuades him from this action?

3. What does Diomedes suggest they do instead?

4. Why does Hera decide to seduce Zeus?

5. What aid does Aphrodite lend her?

6. Who else assists Hera?

7. How does Hera convince him to help her with her plan?

8. How successful is Hera's plan?

9. Who injures Hektor, and how badly is he injured?

10. What happens when Zeus awakens?

Answers

1. Agamemnon, sure of defeat, advises escaping in the ships.

2. Odysseus rather forcefully points out the problem with Agamemnon's plan.

3. Diomedes suggests that while they cannot fight, they can at least encourage the warriors.

4. Hera sees that Poseidon is helping the Achaians, and wants to keep Zeus from finding out.

5. Aphrodite lends Hera her magic Band of Love and Desire.

6. Hera also enlists the help of Sleep.

7. Hera promises Sleep that he can marry one of the Graces, whom he has always admired.

8. Hera easily seduces Zeus, who falls into a deep sleep, and Poseidon is able to help the Achaians push the Trojans back beyond the wall.

9. Aias injures Hektor severely with a large stone, and he seems close to death.

10. Zeus is furious when he sees that the Achaians have rallied and that Hektor is injured. He sends Apollo to strengthen Hektor, and allows the Trojans to push the Achaians back to their ships.

Suggested Essay Topics

1. Examine the power of Zeus as seen in these chapters. What is he capable of controlling? What is he powerless to control? What are his weaknesses? What other examples in the *Iliad* support your claims?

2. Compare Agamemnon's leadership role to Hektor's in this section.

Books Sixteen and Seventeen

New Character:

Automedon: *Achaian warrior who attempts to bring Achilleus' horses into the battle*

Summary

Patroklos brings the grim news that he has heard from Nestor to Achilleus, begging him to put aside his pride and fight to save the Achaians. Failing that, he asks to be allowed to borrow Achilleus' armor and take the Myrmidon army into battle. Achilleus is not ready to forgive Agamemnon, but agrees to send Patroklos in his armor. He instructs Patroklos to come back after driving the Trojans from the ships, lest Achilleus should lose the glory of sacking Troy himself, or a god should come against Patroklos and bring him down.

Meanwhile, the Trojans have succeeded in torching one of the Achaian ships, as Aias could no longer defend it. Achilleus sees the fire and hurries Patroklos on his way, offering libations to Zeus. When the Trojans see Patroklos and the Myrmidon army approaching, they are terrified. Fully believing that Achilleus has given up his anger and is leading the force of fresh warriors, they begin to retreat. Patroklos presses in and kills many Trojans, including Sarpedon, son of Zeus.

After forcing back the Trojans, Patroklos fails to heed Achilleus' instructions and instead presses on in pursuit. As Patroklos and his men are on the brink of taking the city, Apollo steps in and forces him back from the wall. Later, Apollo comes at Patroklos from behind, striking a heavy blow and knocking off his helmet. A Trojan then wounds Patroklos, who attempts to retreat into the Achaian forces. However, when Hektor sees him escaping, he rushes in and mortally wounds him with a spear to his stomach. As Hektor takes the glory for killing such a great warrior, Patroklos tells him that he has not been killed by mortal hands, but by cruel fate. His last words predict the fast approaching death of Hektor at the hand of Achilleus.

When Menelaos sees that Patroklos has been killed, he stands over the body to keep the Trojans from taking the armor. However, he cannot hold back the Trojans by himself, and when he retreats Hektor moves in and takes the armor from the body. Menelaos returns to the body with Aias, and a bitter fight breaks out over the corpse. Apollo urges on the Trojans, and Athene assists the Achaians as both sides attempt to carry the body from the field. When Achilleus' horses learn that their charioteer has been killed

by Hektor, they begin to weep. Automedon drives them into the battle and Hektor, seeing that they are driven by a poor charioteer, unsuccessfully attempts to take them. Patroklos' body is eventually won by the Achaians and taken back to the camp for proper burial, though the general fighting rages on.

Analysis

Achilleus' response to the plea of Patroklos is telling. Just as he sent Patroklos in his place to obtain news of the war from Nestor, he is ready to send Patroklos into battle where he should be going. In sending Patroklos to the battle in his armor, he sentences his companion to death. Achilleus must have known that the Trojans would react strongly to the sight of his armor on the field. Indeed, the mere sight of what they assume to be Achilleus turns the tables to the Achaian advantage. The decision represents a way out for Achilleus. If he sends Patroklos, he can save his own ship, which is in danger of being torched by the Trojans, and he can help the Achaians who are his friends. He can accomplish all of this without giving up an inch in his stubborn stance against Agamemnon. As if that were not bad enough, Achilleus' pride takes him a step further. While the Achaians have been far from home now for nine years as they attempt to sack Troy, Achilleus cannot bear for anyone but himself to take the glory. He instructs Patroklos to quit fighting before the city is taken.

Patroklos is a strong warrior, and he performs very bravely on the field. However, he is not the match of the man who should have been there. Patroklos is ultimately killed, and his death is a direct result of Achilleus' foolish pride. The death of Patroklos is one of a series of tragic events caused by Achilleus that will lead directly to the death of Hektor, which is predicted by Patroklos in his final words, and the death of Achilleus himself.

The vicious fighting for the body of Patroklos underscores the importance of proper burial, and especially the burial of a warrior hero. While many have died on the battlefield, only a few of the very bravest warriors receive the treatment given to Patroklos. Earlier, the epic tells of a break in the fighting to burn the bodies of many dead. Patroklos, however, will receive elaborate individual attention. The fighting over the body may also be heightened by the Achaian's awareness of the warrior's tie to Achilleus. They must realize that such a death will not be taken lightly by the great hero. The responsibility of man to man here does not end with death. Each man trusts his friends to also provide proper burial for his body and thus usher him safely into the underworld. In order to do this, the body must be retrieved.

The response of Achilleus' horses to the death of Patroklos is a vivid example of personification. Homer imbues the horses with the very human emotions of grief and sadness. Their reaction is similar to the reaction you would expect to see from a close friend. The effect is to powerfully underscore the loss of a great man.

Study Questions

1. Does Achilleus agree to end his grudge against Agamemnon at the request of Patroklos? Why?

2. What does Achilleus agree to do?

3. What are Achilleus' instructions to Patroklos?

4. Why does he tell Patroklos to limit his efforts?

5. What event makes Achilleus hurry Patroklos on his way?

6. What happens when the Trojans see Patroklos and the Myrmidon army approaching?

7. Who intervenes when Patroklos is on the verge of taking the city?

8. Who finally kills Patroklos?

9. Why is there such fierce fighting over the body of Patroklos?

10. How do Achilleus' horses react to the death of Patroklos?

Answers

1. No, Achilleus is not ready to put aside his pride and reconcile with Agamemnon.

2. Achilleus agrees to send Patroklos out with the Myrmidon forces in his armor.

3. Achilleus instructs Patroklos to push back the Trojans, but not to take the city.

4. Achilleus tells Patroklos not to take Troy because he wants the glory for himself.

5. The Trojans succeed in torching one of the Achaian ships.

6. The Trojans are afraid when they see the Myrmidons and what appears to be Achilleus, and they begin to retreat.

7. Apollo intervenes and pushes Patroklos back from the Trojan wall, knocking off his helmet.

8. Hektor kills Patroklos after he has been wounded by another Trojan.

9. The Achaians fight fiercely for the body of Patroklos in order to give it a proper burial.

10. The horses weep at the death of Patroklos.

Suggested Essay Topics

1. Trace the effects of Achilleus' decision to send Patroklos out onto the battlefield in his armor. What does he seek to gain by doing so? How does this incident illuminate his fatal flaw? What events are directly caused by this decision?

2. What are the immediate reactions caused by the death of Patroklos? What do they tell us about Patroklos as a warrior and as a man?

Book Eighteen

Summary

Antilochos brings the news of Patroklos' death to Achilleus, who is distraught with grief. He pours dust and ashes over his head and sprawls on the ground tearing at his hair. As everyone in the hut weeps for Patroklos, Achilleus utters a terrible cry of mourning. Thetis hears his cry and goes to comfort him. Achilleus tells his mother that Hektor must pay with his life for the death of Patroklos. His mother tells him that his own death is fated to follow directly after Hektor's, but Achilleus will not be dissuaded. However, Achilleus no longer has his armor and cannot go into battle unarmed. Thetis agrees to have a new set of armor made by Hephaistos in Olympus, and instructs Achilleus to do nothing until she returns in the morning.

Back on the battlefield, the Trojans are pushing the Achaians back to their ships, and they catch up to the body of Patroklos. Again, the two armies fight fiercely over the body. Hera sends Iris down from Olympus to rouse Achilleus to defend Patroklos. She instructs him to go out to the ditch and show himself to the Trojans to hold off their fighting. Athene wraps Achilleus in the aegis, and he is surrounded by a blazing light. As he stands at the ditch, he utters three fierce shouts that carry loud and clear to the Trojans, striking them with terror. As the Trojans are thrown into confusion, the Achaians are able to drag Patroklos out of the fighting.

As evening falls and the fighting ceases, the Trojans hold a strategy council. Poulydamas again warns Hektor to retreat, fearing the wrath of Achilleus. Better to be within the city walls where it will be easier to defend the city. Yet again, Hektor rejects his advice. The Trojans approve Hektor's plan to keep fighting.

The Achaians spend the night mourning Patroklos. Achilleus swears that Patroklos will not be buried until the armor and head of Hektor have been captured and the throats of 12 Trojan children have been cut in revenge. The body is washed and anointed and laid on a bier.

Thetis reaches Olympus and convinces the lame god Hephaistos to craft beautiful armor for her son. He produces a shield depicting many beautiful scenes of both war and peace, a corselet, a heavy helmet, and greaves of tin. When the armor is finished, Thetis carries it to her son.

Analysis

The full implication of Achilleus' plan to revenge the death of Patroklos is spelled out by Thetis. If he chooses to kill Hektor, it is fated that his death will soon follow. Achilleus is thus given a choice. If he chooses not to kill Hektor, he may live to return to his home. If he chooses to make Hektor pay for Patroklos' death with his own, he will not leave the battlefields of Troy alive. Achilleus' love for Patroklos, and his sense of responsibility for his death, are so great that he cannot walk away without revenge. In killing Hektor,

Achilleus also hopes to break the strength of the Trojans by taking out their leader, and to reduce his own feelings of guilt.

Achilleus' reactions to the news of Patroklos' death are an interesting picture of the customs of the culture. He tears out clumps of his hair and covers his head with dust, writhing on the ground and moaning loudly. Achilleus is not the only one moaning. All of the women in the household, as well as many others, join in the wailing. Each of these actions serves as an outlet for the enormous emotional response to the death of a close friend. Many men have died on the battlefield before Patroklos, but none has stirred such a reaction among the survivors. This is due partly to Patroklos' status as a great warrior, but the excessive grief stems mostly from the reaction of Achilleus. Achilleus is at the center of all the mourning and funeral rituals. Again, he is driven by his great love for Patroklos, but also by his guilt.

Fearing the extreme reaction of Achilleus to the death of Patroklos, Poulydamas again advises Hektor to fall back. As Poulydamas speaks with the voice of reason. Hektor, however, refuses to listen to reason. All along he has shown a strong belief in fate. If it is fated for him or any other Trojan to die, they will die. Armed with this tenet, as well as with his deep sense of responsibility, he charges ahead.

The transfiguration of Achilleus is another example of the fire imagery prevalent in the epic. Flames of fire appear to shoot from the warrior's head, symbolizing the destruction and burning of a great city. The image foreshadows the fall of Troy.

Study Questions

1. How does Achilleus react to the news of the death of Patroklos?

2. Who hears Achilleus' tortured cry of grief?

3. What does Thetis tell Achilleus about his fate?

4. What is Achilleus' response to this revelation?

5. What stops Achilleus from going out immediately to fight Hektor?

6. What is Thetis' solution to this problem?

7. What does Hera instruct Achilleus to do for the Achaians in the meantime?

8. How can Achilleus do this without any armor?

9. What are the Achaians able to do as a result?

10. What does Poulydamas advise Hektor to do, and what is his response?

Answers

1. Achilleus is distraught, and covers himself with dust, tearing out his hair.

2. Thetis hears his cry and comes to comfort him.

3. Thetis tells Achilleus that if he kills Hektor, his own death will shortly follow.

4. Achilleus is bent on revenge regardless of the consequences.

5. Achilleus cannot go into battle without his armor, which Hektor has taken.

6. Thetis offers to go to Olympus and have Hephaistos make a new suit of armor.

7. Hera sends Iris to instruct Achilleus to go out to the ditch and show himself to the Trojans.

8. Athene surrounds Achilleus with a blazing light. As he stands at the ditch, he utters three fierce shouts that strike the Trojans with terror.

9. In the resulting confusion, the Achaians are able to drag Patroklos' body out of the fighting.

10. Poulydamas is fearful of Achilleus' reaction to the death of Patroklos and advises Hektor to retreat behind the city walls for protection. Hektor refuses to retreat.

Suggested Essay Topics

1. Describe the mourning process as seen in Achilleus' reaction to the death of Patroklos. What other examples of similar behavior are shown in the *Iliad*? How are they different from modern America's customs of mourning?

2.   Achilleus has a mortal father and an immortal mother. What
     effect does this have on his actions? What are the advantages
     and disadvantages of this parentage?

Book Nineteen

New Character:

Xanthos: *Achilleus' horse, who prophesies his coming death*

Summary

Thetis brings the new armor to Achilleus and finds him still
weeping over the body of Patroklos. Achilleus takes his new armor
and gathers the Achaians together. He announces that he is putting aside his anger toward Agamemnon and that he will now return to the battle. This news is greeted with joy by the Achaians.
Agamemnon then answers Achilleus, acknowledging the folly of
their quarrel and again offering the great gifts he had promised.

Achilleus is eager to do battle and urges the Achaians to ready
themselves without delay. Odysseus points out that the men have
not eaten, and that they will need strength for the battle. He suggests that first they rest and feast, and that Agamemnon bring the
gifts for Achilleus for all to see. Achilleus relents, but swears that
he will neither eat nor drink until he has avenged the death of
Patroklos. The gifts are brought out to Achilleus and a great oath is
sworn before Zeus that Agamemnon did not lie with Briseis.

Achilleus puts on his new armor and mounts his chariot, call-
ing out to his horses to bring him home safely, unlike Patroklos.
The horse Xanthos speaks back to him, assuring him that he will
return from this day's battle unharmed. He goes on, however, to
predict the fated death of Achilleus. This angers Achilleus, as he
well knows his death is near. He is determined nonetheless to drive
back the Trojans, and with a loud shout he sets off for battle.

Analysis

Achilleus finally reconciles with Agamemnon. However, the
decision does not stem from any moral revelation of his foolish
pride. Rather, he is moved by the motive of revenge for Patroklos.

His speech about putting aside his quarrel with Agamemnon seems only a formality that will allow him to join in the battle. He shows how little he is interested in the new peace with Agamemnon by brushing off the leader's attempts to bring him gifts. Achilleus again shows he has no interest in material possessions. Clearly his mind is focused only on finding Hektor and making him pay for his actions.

Achilleus takes the further step of refusing to eat or drink until Hektor has been killed. This move serves to isolate him from the larger forces. It is clear that avenging Patroklos' death will be his mission, and not an Achaian group effort. Achilleus chooses not to join in the camaraderie of the feasting. This decision is due to his enormous sense of grief and the unyielding concentration he has on his mission. However, it seems to slight Agamemnon's offers of hospitality. By refusing nourishment, Achilleus is also showing that nothing, not even life itself, matters to him as much as his dear friend. Eating and drinking are fundamental human needs. In refusing them, he becomes superhuman, accepting strength from Athene.

In a bizarre attempt to "pass the buck," Achilleus blames his horses for not bringing Patroklos back alive. Achilleus is desperately trying to escape his own guilty feelings for the death of his friend. In an equally bizarre exchange, one of the horses answers him. The horse tells Achilleus that the death was the result of Apollo's actions and the hand of fate. There is a very real tension here between human decisions and their inevitable consequences, and the role played by fate. Hektor continually acts without concern for consequences, sure of the knowledge that fate will run its course regardless of his decisions. Achilleus, however, struggles with the guilt of having made a decision that had tragic results. There would be no room for guilt if all were dependent on fate. Achilleus sees room for bending fate, and is actually given a choice that will save him from his fated death for a time. In his grief, however, he has no desire to prolong his life.

Study Questions

1. Why does Achilleus reconcile with Agamemnon?

2. What does Agamemnon offer Achilleus?

3. What does Agamemnon want to do after the reconciliation?

4. What does Achilleus want to do?

5. What does Achilleus say he will not do until Hektor is killed?

6. What do the Achaians decide to do next?

7. How does Achilleus obtain strength for the battle?

8. Whom does Achilleus chastise for their role in the death of Patroklos?

9. What is the response?

10. What is said that angers Achilleus?

Answers

1. Achilleus reconciles with Agamemnon because he is intent on avenging the death of Patroklos.

2. Agamemnon offers Achilleus all the gifts that he had previously offered.

3. Agamemnon wants to bring out all the gifts for Achilleus and hold a large feast.

4. Achilleus is eager to get to the battle immediately.

5. Achilleus swears he will not eat or drink until Patroklos' death is avenged.

6. The gifts are brought to Achilleus, and the Achaians hold a feast to strengthen themselves for the battle.

7. Athene gives him strength for the battle.

8. Achilleus reproaches his horses for not bringing Patroklos home alive.

9. One of the horses speaks to Achilleus, stating that it was not their fault that Patroklos died.

10. The horse prophesies the death of Achilleus. Achilleus responds that he is aware of his fate, but determined to avenge the death of Patroklos anyway.

Suggested Essay Topics

1. How does Achilleus learn of his final fate? How many times does he hear of it? Does he have the power to change his fate in any way?

2. What is the significance of feasting in the *Iliad*? When are feasts held? Why does Achilleus refuse to attend Agamemnon's feast in this book?

Books Twenty and Twenty-one

New Characters:

Asteropaios: *Trojan warrior who faces Achilleus at the river's edge*

Aganor: *Trojan who keeps Achilleus from taking Troy*

Summary

As the Achaians and the Trojans arm themselves, Zeus calls the gods together in Olympus. Zeus orders the gods to enter the battle on whichever side they choose. He is afraid that Achilleus, in his anger, will overstep fate and storm the walls of Troy. The gods quickly join their favored sides as battle begins.

Aineias, spurred on by Apollo, challenges Achilleus. When the fierce duel approaches its destined conclusion, Poseidon fears for Aineias and rushes in to spirit the warrior away from the field. Though Poseidon is aiding the Achaians, he knows that it is fated that Aineias should survive and carry on Priam's line as king of the Trojans. Achilleus sees that the gods have rescued Aineias and turns to kill many other Trojans. After Achilleus kills Hektor's brother Polydoros, the Trojan prince attacks him, but Apollo wraps Hektor in a thick mist to keep Achilleus from killing him.

As Book Twenty-one opens, Achilleus has forced the Trojans into full retreat in two groups. One group runs toward the city and the other runs right into the river Xanthos. Achilleus leaps into the river with his sword and kills a great number of Trojans, sparing 12 young men alive to fulfill his promise to Patroklos. Lykaon begs for his life at the river's edge, but Achilleus shows no mercy.

Meanwhile, the river Xanthos is growing ever angrier at
Achilleus for the Trojans' destruction. Xanthos gives courage to
Asteropaios to challenge Achilleus. Asteropaios succeeds in wound-
ing his elbow, but pays with his life. Then the river addresses
Achilleus, imploring him to stop his rampage, as the river is choked
with corpses. Achilleus agrees to move away from the river, but
refuses to stop killing the Trojans. The river then rushes at Achilleus,
whipping up its water and beating on him with great waves.
Poseidon and Athene come to Achilleus to reassure him that he
will not die at the hands of the river and to advise him to keep
pushing the Trojans until they are inside the walls of the city. Then

Hera and Hephaistos rescue Achilleus by sending a great fire onto the river to dry up the water and force Xanthos to relent.

Meanwhile, the gods fight each other with a great crash as Athene brings down Ares and Aphrodite. Apollo refuses a challenge from Poseidon out of respect for his uncle. Hera takes on Artemis, who runs from the field in tears and complains to her father Zeus.

Priam sees the Trojans running in terror from Achilleus and has the city doors thrown open to receive them. Apollo puts courage in Agenor's heart to face Achilleus and give the rest of the Trojan's time to get behind the city walls. Agenor is no match for Achilleus, and before he is killed, Apollo snatches him away out of the battle. Apollo then tricks Achilleus into thinking he himself is Agenor, and Achilleus chases him far off down the plain, away from the city walls, as the Trojans escape safely behind them.

Analysis

Zeus' meeting with the gods reveals another clue about the role of fate in the *Iliad*. Rather than being an inescapable blueprint of life's events, it seems that men are capable of acting contrary to fate. The role of the gods here is to police men so that they act within their fate. Zeus allows all of the gods to intervene as they choose in order to avoid allowing Achilleus to overstep fate and destroy Troy before the appointed time.

There are other revelations of fate in this chapter as well: Aineias, while close to death, is visited by Poseidon, who tells him he is fated to survive. If only he will avoid conflict with Achilleus, no other Achaian will kill him. Again, the possibility of fate changing is left open. Should Aineias confront Achilleus, he would not survive the battle. Interestingly, Poseidon is on the side of the Achaians, thus it is odd for him to save a Trojan. Apparently, Poseidon's knowledge of Aineias' fate forces his hand. Likewise, Apollo warns Hektor not to face Achilleus out in the open or he will surely be killed. Again, there is a choice to be made. In Hektor's case, he chooses to disregard the advice of Apollo and must be rescued by Apollo when he foolishly rushes in to face Achilleus. In Hektor's case, however, we know that he is merely buying himself some time. In both of these cases, it seems likely that without intervention by the immortals, the men would have died before their fated times. The gods' actions are crucial to the workings of fate. The pattern repeats itself a third time when Agenor faces Achilleus. At the last moment, Agenor is whisked away from danger by Apollo, who takes his place. Again, it seems the gods are directing fate.

The river Xanthos is another dramatic example of personification. The river is given the ability to speak and the very human emotions of anger and pity. Even more remarkable, however, is the ability of the river to act completely beyond its natural scope and physically attack Achilleus. The river is actually one of the immortals. As such, it has the power to drag Achilleus under and bring him to his death. Without the intervention of Hera and Hephaistos, Achilleus would not have survived. The act of controlling the river with fire is an inversion of the common controlling of fire with water.

Study Questions

1. Why does Zeus reverse his previous warning and invite the gods to intervene?

2. What is the outcome of the duel between Aineias and Achilleus?

3. Why does Poseidon act in this way?

4. What warning does Apollo give Hektor regarding Achilleus?

5. Does he act accordingly?

6. How does Hektor survive the duel?

7. Why does Achilleus take 12 young Trojan warriors as prisoners?

8. What is the river's reaction to all the Trojans killed in its waters?

9. How does Achilleus escape?

10. What is the outcome of the duel between Agenor and Achilleus?

Answers

1. Zeus is afraid that Achilleus will overstep the bounds of fate.

2. The duel ends when Aineias is spirited away by Poseidon.

3. Poseidon knows that Aineias is not fated to die at that time.

4. Apollo warns Hektor that he will die if he challenges Achilleus

in the open.

5. Hektor refuses to heed the warning and challenges Achilleus anyway.

6. Apollo wraps Hektor in a thick mist to keep Achilleus from killing him.

7. Achilleus takes 12 young Trojans to fulfill his promise to Patroklos that they would be killed at his bier as part of the revenge for his death.

8. The river is furious with Achilleus and attacks him, attempting to drown him.

9. Achilleus escapes the river when Hera and Hephaistos send fire to dry up the water.

10. Apollo whisks Agenor away before Achilleus can kill him. He disguises himself as Agenor and leads Achilleus away from the Trojan wall so the Trojans can safely retreat behind it.

Suggested Essay Topics

1. How do the gods intervene in this chapter to insure that fate is served? How might the ending of the *Iliad* have differed had the gods not intervened here?

2. Trace the image of fire through the epic. What are its different forms? What are its meanings?

Book Twenty-two

New Character:

Deiphobos: *brother of Hektor, whose form Athene takes in fooling Hektor*

Summary

As the other Trojans recover from the battle behind the city walls, Hektor remains alone outside the city to face Achilleus. Apollo then reveals himself. Achilleus is furious with the trick and moves quickly back to the city. Priam sees him coming and begs his son to reconsider and come inside the walls. His mother then adds her entreaties, but neither can convince him to give up his post. Hektor goes over his options. He can give up and go back into the city, where he will surely be blamed for the destruction of his people. He can put down his armor and meet Achilleus unarmed, offering to return Helen and give great treasure along with her. However, Achilleus would probably kill him regardless. He decides his best option is fighting.

As Achilleus nears Hektor, the Trojan's courage fails, and he begins to retreat in terror. Achilleus relentlessly chases Hektor around the city walls as the Trojan tries unsuccessfully to dash for the gates and get inside. As they complete three full laps around the city, Zeus holds up his golden scales and puts a fate of death in each pan. When Hektor's doom sinks down, Apollo leaves him to his fate.

Athene then appears to Hektor in the guise of Deiphobos, one of his brothers. Believing that he will have help in fighting Achilleus, Hektor turns to face him. He swears that if Achilleus is slain, his body will be returned to the Achaians, and requests a similar oath from Achilleus. Achilleus, however, refuses to make any promises.

The two begin their duel, and Hektor soon discovers that Deiphobos is not there and that the gods have brought him to his certain death. After several unsuccessful attempts by both men, Achilleus finds a vulnerable point at Hektor's collarbone and drives a spear through his neck. As Hektor takes his last breaths, he beseeches Achilleus again to give his body to his father in exchange for great ransom. Again, Achilleus refuses, and Hektor dies predicting Achilleus' death at the hands of Paris and Apollo.

The other Achaians rush to see the body of the mighty Hektor, and many stab the corpse. Achilleus strips the body and attaches it by the feet to his chariot. As he speeds back to the ships, the body is dragged behind in the dust, defiled.

Hektor's parents are overcome with grief for their son's death; they weep and moan loudly. The other Trojans join them in their cries, and eventually the sound carries to Andromache. She rushes out to find the reason for the wailing. As she hears of Hektor's death, she faints. The book ends with the Trojan women mourning their fallen leader.

Analysis

The character of Hektor is vividly revealed in his final choice of action. A lesser man would have hidden behind the wall with the rest of the Trojans. Instead, Hektor takes on the responsibility of defending his city in a fateful encounter with Achilleus. Hektor has consistently acted without thought of personal danger, secure in the knowledge that fate will be served, and this instance is no exception. In deciding to fight, Hektor turns his back on two options that might have saved his life. He could have escaped behind the wall. He could also have approached Achilleus unarmed, offering the return of Helen and much treasure. Hektor, however, is bound by the heroic code to defend his city.

Hektor does briefly lose his composure when faced with the sight of Achilleus bent on revenge. The vision of Achilleus in his immortal armor must have been terrifying to send such a brave man running. Hektor's flight around the city gives the Trojans an opportunity to help him by attacking Achilleus from the wall. In this culture, a warrior will normally fight only if he has a reasonable chance to win. If he feels that he is no match for the opponent, he will simply run away. There is no disgrace in Hektor's running. However, there is no escaping fate, and Hektor cannot escape the duel with Achilleus. Again, the gods step in, not to create a supernatural event, but to encourage what was fated to happen anyway. Athene fools Hektor into thinking he will have help in fighting Achilleus. Her choice of disguises is wise, only his brother would risk death for him. Once Hektor realizes fate has turned against him, he faces Achilleus and fights bravely.

The words exchanged during the duel reveal the contrast between Achilleus and Hektor. While Hektor offers to treat Achilleus' body with respect if he is the one killed, Achilleus will make no comparable promise. While much of the gesture can be explained by the fact that Hektor believes he will be the one destroyed, the act still shows his nature. Achilleus is blinded by rage, mad with grief, starving, and sleepless. The Achaian is bound by his code of honor to avenge Patroklos, yet he knows that means he is giving up his own life as well. He seems almost inhuman as he meets his enemy. Hektor, however, remains very human, showing a range of emotions from despair to hope to ultimate resignation. Hektor is the only character that appears in every single book of the *Iliad*, and Homer has developed this character more than any other. The full depth of that development is revealed in his final living moments.

As Hektor dies, he is again denied his request of a proper family burial. Achilleus once more pushes himself to the extreme. Just as he refused to reconcile with Agamemnon before he was completely humiliated, so he will not be swerved from his path of revenge, even after killing Hektor. In full view of the Trojans watching from the wall, Achilleus defiles Hektor's dead body by dragging it from the back of his chariot. There is no pity and no remorse.

. Achilleus' treatment of the body is the culmination of the mutilation theme that has run throughout the epic. While mutilation has been threatened over and over, there are no other examples of such ill treatment in the poem. Mutilation of corpses was actually a common practice in the time period, and the *Iliad* is unique in that it does not describe more such abominations. While there are battles fought over bodies and we can assume that they were not treated kindly if won by the other side, we are never privy to the details. The effect is a powerful focus on the horror of the act as described in this book.

Study Questions

1. What are Hektor's options as Achilleus approaches the gates of Troy?

2. Which option does he choose?

3. Who tries to dissuade him?

4. What does Hektor do as he sees Achilleus approaching?

5. Who intervenes?

6. How does she cause Hektor to stand up to fight Achilleus?

7. What promise does Hektor make to Achilleus?

8. Does Achilleus promise the same?

9. What does Hektor ask as he dies?

10. What happens to Hektor's body?

Answers

1. Hektor can escape behind the walls of the city, face Achilleus unarmed while offering gifts, or stand up to fight him.

2. Hektor chooses to stay and fight.

3. Both his mother and his father attempt to convince him to come inside the walls.

4. Hektor loses his courage and flees, running around the city three times.

5. Athene intervenes.

6. Athene takes the form of Hektor's brother and leads him to believe that he will have help in fighting Achilleus.

7. Hektor promises that if he kills Achilleus, his body will be returned to the Achaians for proper burial.

8. Achilleus refuses to promise the return of Hektor's body. He is bent on revenge.

9. Hektor again requests that his body be returned to his parents for burial.

10. Hektor's body is first stabbed by many of the Achaians, then attached by the ankles to Achilleus' chariot and dragged behind it.

Suggested Essay Topics

1. Compare Hektor's final actions and emotions to those of Achilleus before the fight. What are the competing codes of honor shown in this sequence? What values does each man symbolize?

2. How might the ending have been different if Hektor had chosen one of the other two options? Why is he unable to do so?

Book Twenty-three

Summary

The Achaians return to their ships, and Achilleus and the Myrmidons immediately resume their mourning of Patroklos. They drive their chariots around his body three times and defile the body of Hektor. Then they take off their armor and hold a great funeral feast. As Achilleus falls asleep on the beach, the ghost of Patroklos appears to him. The ghost admonishes him for not properly burying his body and thus preventing his spirit's passage through the gates of Hades. He also requests that his bones and Achilleus' be placed together in death as they were together in life.

In the morning men are sent to gather wood for the funeral pyre. Achilleus orders the Myrmidons to arm themselves, and Patroklos' body is carried to the pyre site. Achilleus cuts off the lock of hair he had been growing in dedication to the river Spercheios for his safe return. The pyre is built 100 feet square and the body is placed on top. The body is wrapped in the fat of sheep and cattle, and their carcasses are added to the pyre. Along with these are added jars of honey and oil, four horses, two dogs, and the 12 captured Trojans, and the pyre is set aflame. After the fire has done its work, it is extinguished with wine. The bones of Patroklos are carefully separated from the others and gathered in a golden jar for burial. A mound is built over the site of the pyre as a memorial.

Meanwhile, Aphrodite protects the corpse of Hektor, keeping the dogs away and anointing his skin to protect it from tearing. Apollo brings a dark cloud over the body to keep the sun from damaging it.

After the proper burial procedures for Patroklos have been followed, Achilleus gathers the people and shows them the prizes to be offered in the funeral games. There is to be a great chariot race, a boxing fight, a wrestling match, a foot race, a duel, a discus competition, an archery competition, and a spear throw. The competition is fierce but civil, and all the prizes are awarded.

Analysis

Ironically, after all that Achilleus has done for Patroklos, the ghost of his friend admonishes Achilleus for forgetting him. The appearance of the ghost of Patroklos underlines the importance of proper burial. While Achilleus has been doing everything in his power to mourn Patroklos and revenge his death, he has not actually buried the remains. Because of this, the spirit of the dead man is forced to wander around the gates of Hades without entering. The peaceful passage of the soul into the afterlife depends very heavily on the actions of the living.

Those actions are described in detail in this chapter. The funeral pyre is enormous, and it takes many men to gather the wood. Elaborate measures are taken to purify the body. First it is carefully washed, then anointed with oils and wrapped in fat. Finally, the body is burned. The dead man is treated as if he were embarking on a long journey, and several things are burned along with the body to make the traveling more comfortable. These include jars of honey and oil for sustenance, and horses and dogs for companionship. The 12 captured Trojans who burned with Patroklos are for revenge, and also sent to serve the warrior in the afterlife. Just as war prisoners are sold or given into slavery in life, so they are given in death.

The cutting of Achilleus' hair is symbolic of his dedication to his dead comrade. The hair was grown to honor the river Spercheios in anticipation of a safe return. However, Achilleus has now made the decision to avenge Patroklos, knowing that killing Hektor will bring about his own death. Because hair continues to grow after

death, it becomes a symbol for life. The death of Patroklos has blocked out everything else for Achilleus. His life has lost its meaning. When Achilleus cuts his hair, he is both acknowledging that he will not return to his homeland alive and symbolically sending his own life to the flames in the ultimate gesture of mourning.

Another important funeral ritual includes the games held in the dead warrior's memory. As the dead man showed his bravery and skill in battle, so those who remain compete in tests of strength. The prizes offered by Achilleus are elaborate. The events comprise a sort of Olympics, as the men compete in races, discus throwing, boxing, and other sports. The games serve as an opportunity to reunite Achilles with the community. His self-imposed isolation from the Achaians is over now that Patroklos has been avenged. His offering of such generous prizes shows his good will to the others and almost serves as an apology for his past behavior.

Study Questions

1. What do the Myrmidons do after returning to their camp?
2. Who appears to Achilleus in his dream?
3. What is his message?
4. What does Patroklos request that Achilleus do with his bones?
5. Why does Achilleus cut off his hair?
6. What is the significance of the act?
7. What is burned on the pyre with Patroklos?
8. Why are these items added to the pyre?
9. Why has Hektor's body not disintegrated under the harsh treatment of Achilleus?
10. Why does Achilleus hold the funeral games?

Answers

1. They ride around the funeral pyre three times, defiling the body of Hektor.
2. The ghost of Patroklos appears to Achilleus as he sleeps.

3. The ghost admonishes Achilleus for not giving his body proper burial.

4. Patroklos asks Achilleus to have both of their bones buried together.

5. Achilleus cuts his hair to honor the memory of Patroklos, and burns it along with the body.

6. Achilleus was growing the lock as a gift to the river Spercheios in exchange for his safe return from battle. He now realizes he will not return alive.

7. Jars of honey and oil, four horses, two dogs, and the 12 captured Trojans are burned.

8. The items are added to grant Patroklos sustenance, companionship, and service in the underworld.

9. Apollo and Aphrodite have been preserving Hektor's body.

10. The funeral games are held to honor Achilleus' dead friend by simulating his brave acts in battle. They also help to assimilate Achilleus back into the community.

Suggested Essay Topics

1. Explore the importance of the proper burial of a hero as described in the *Iliad*. What steps are taken, and why? What happens if these steps are not followed?

2. Describe each item that is burned on the pyre with Patroklos. What is the significance of each item? How is it used in life? How will it help in death?

Book Twenty-four

Summary

Achilleus is so overwhelmed with grief for his friend that he cannot sleep. Each night he rises and ties Hektor's body to his chariot, driving his horses around Patroklos' tomb three times. Still, the gods protect the corpse, and it does not degenerate.

The gods begin to argue over the body of Hektor, some wanting to steal it away from Achilleus for proper burial, and some having no pity for the Trojan. Finally, Zeus tells Hera that Hektor, too, was dear to the gods. He sends Thetis to Achilleus to tell him that Zeus is enraged at his behavior and that he must return Hektor's body to Priam.

Another messenger is sent to Priam, urging him to take great ransom to Achilleus in exchange for Hektor's body. Against his wife's advice, Priam gathers gifts of great value and makes his way into the Achaian camp with Hermes as his protector. When he reaches Achilleus, Priam makes an impassioned plea for his son's body, reminding Achilleus of his own father. Both men are moved to tears, and Achilleus agrees to give up the body. Achilleus orders his serving-women to wash and anoint Hektor's body and wrap it in a beautiful cloak. A meal is prepared and a bed is laid down for Priam. Achilleus agrees to a request for a 12-day reprieve from the fighting in order to give Hektor a proper burial. Then all of the Achaians sleep, and Hermes spirits Priam out of the camp unseen.

The Trojans come out of the city to meet Priam, weeping uncontrollably. Hektor's body is brought into the city and dirges are sung for him. Hektor's wife and mother, as well as Helen, all pour out their grief, lamenting their loss. The Trojans then spend nine days gathering wood, and on the tenth day they set Hektor's body on the pyre and burn it. The next day the fire is extinguished with wine and the bones are gathered and buried. A mound is built up over the grave and a vast feast is given in the house of Priam.

Analysis

Achilleus' harsh treatment of the body of Hektor is made all the more horrible because it follows the description of the elaborate care taken with Patroklos. Achilleus has had his revenge and he should give up his anger against Hektor. Instead, his actions are extreme and demonstrate his stubbornness. He handles his revenge exactly the way he handled his anger with Agamemnon. In his fury, he has dishonored the earth, and has invoked the anger of the gods. Achilleus has obviously learned nothing from his experience, despite the tragic consequences.

The moral insight finally comes when Achilleus meets with Priam. In speaking with the old man, Achilleus is reminded of the depth of his love for his own father, and the fact that he will not live to see him again. Both men weep for what they have lost. For Achilleus, these things include his father and his dear friend Patroklos, his home, and his future. For Priam they include Hektor, his other sons killed in battle, and most likely the security of his city and home life. In this scene, Achilleus becomes fully human as he connects emotionally with Priam and finally shows some pity and decency. This scene is the climax of the epic. In agreeing to return Hektor's body to his father, Achilleus finally puts aside his anger and pride.

The impact of Priam on Achilleus is striking. Part of the effect is certainly the shock of seeing the Trojan king at the door. Priam's sudden appearance breaks the thought patterns of Achilleus, shattering any prejudice, fear, or suspicion. The two enemies represent two worlds coming together. There is no longer any distinction between friend and foe, and there is no talk of right or wrong. When these men weep they weep not just for Hektor and for Patroklos, but for the tragedy of all mankind. When they quit their weeping to feast, they acknowledge that life must continue, though it exists simultaneously with sorrow. This recognition of mortality is a central theme of the *Iliad* that culminates in these final pages.

Homer brings the *Iliad* to a close with the burial of Hektor. The ending seems almost too abrupt. Knowing that Achilleus is destined to die and Troy to fall to the Achaians, the reader wants to know how it happens. Homer leaves him guessing. The effect of the ending the way it stands is a final note of forgiveness and dignity rather than tragedy and bloodshed. Had Homer ended with the fall of Troy, or with the death of Achilleus, the feeling would have been of despair and hopelessness. Instead there is a sense of hope. Achilleus has come to moral redemption, and a wrong done has been righted. The *Iliad* is, fundamentally, the story of Achilleus, and ends appropriately with his moral transformation.

Study Questions

1. What does Achilleus do each night to the body of Hektor?

2. Why does he anger the gods?

3. Who do the gods send as a messenger to Achilleus, and what is the message?

4. What does Priam bring to Achilleus?

5. How does Priam move safely through the Achaian camp to Achilleus?

6. What does Priam talk about that moves Achilleus to tears?

7. What is the climactic scene of the *Iliad*?

8. What do the two men agree to do about the fighting?

9. What kind of burial is given to Hektor?

10. Why does the *Iliad* end with the burial of Hektor?

Answers

1. Achilleus ties the body of Hektor to his chariot and drags it around Patroklos' grave.

2. The gods are angry that he shows no pity or decency and that he is defiling the earth.

3. The gods send Thetis to convince Achilleus to surrender Hektor's body to Priam.

4. Priam brings many valuable gifts as ransom for the body of Hektor.

5. Hermes goes with Priam as his protector and delivers him safely to Achilleus' hut.

6. Priam reminds Achilleus of his own father and moves him to tears.

7. The climax of the *Iliad* occurs when Achilleus agrees to return Hektor's body to Priam, showing his ultimate humanity and moral redemption.

8. A 12-day reprieve in the fighting is agreed upon in order to properly bury Hektor.

9. The Trojans prepare a burial for Hektor nearly identical to that of Patroklos.

10. The *Iliad* ends with the burial of Hektor to emphasize the moral redemption of Achilleus rather than the destruction and tragedy of his death or the fall of Troy.

Suggested Essay Topics

1. Describe the changes that take place in Achilleus during his meeting with Priam. How has he learned from his tragedy? How is Priam able to bring about this change of heart? Where do Achilleus' old habits show themselves?

2. Compare Chryses as a father in Book One to Priam as a father in Book Twenty-four. How are the two similar? How do their stories serve to frame the theme of the *Iliad*?

Sample Analytical Paper Topics

Topic #1

The gods are discussed in the *Iliad* nearly as much as the mortals, and their actions are vital to the plot. Analyze the role of the gods throughout the work using specific examples to support your conclusions.

Outline

I. Thesis Statement: *The gods in the **Iliad** serve as the instruments of fate, stepping into the mortal arena when necessary to insure that fate's purposes are served.*

II. The nature of fate as seen in the *Iliad*

    A. Zeus' scales of fate

    B. Actions with inevitable consequences

    C. Danger of overstepping fate

III. The gods' interaction with men

    A. Gods sent as messengers to mortals to influence decisions

    B. Revelations of fate to mortals by gods

    C. Whisking of warriors away from danger

IV. Limitations put on the gods by fate

    A. The desires of the gods that are sometimes in conflict with fate

B. Gods deceiving and defying Zeus, and the consequences

Topic #2

Achilleus, Agamemnon, and Hektor each represent different values. Compare and contrast the motivations of each warrior, discussing how their point of reference determines their actions.

Outline

I. Thesis Statement: *While every character in the* **Iliad** *is bound by the heroic code, the motivations behind their actions are very different. Achilleus, Agamemnon, and Hektor each represent different value systems and world views.*

II. The heroic code as seen in the *Iliad*

    A. The bond of friendship

    B. The customs of hospitality

    C. The concept of loyalty and courage in battle

III. The motivations of Agamemnon

    A. Position as leader of the Achaian forces and fierce, unfeeling warrior

    B. Loyalty to his brother Menelaos

    C. Power struggles and skirmish with Achilleus

    D. Offers of reconciliation and when they are made

IV. The motivations of Achilleus

    A. Position as greatest of the Achaian warriors

    B. Loyalty to Patroklos

    C. Pride and stubbornness

V. The motivations of Hektor

    A. Position as leader of the Trojan forces

    B. Responsibility and attempting to instill it in Paris

    C. Influences of home and family

Topic #3

There are many women characters included in the narrative of the *Iliad*, some mortal and some immortal. Explore the role of these female characters and their purpose in the scope of the work.

Outline

I.   Thesis Statement: *In the culture of the **Iliad**, mortal women are treated as property rather than human beings. While the gods attempt to treat the goddesses the same way, the goddesses are quick to assert themselves and claim equal power.*

II.   Mortal women as war prizes

    A.   Briseis

    B.   Chryseis

    C.   Fear of the Trojans

III.   Mortal women as gifts

    A.   Agamemnon's gifts to Chryses

    B.   Agamemnon's gifts to Achilleus

IV.   Zeus' treatment of the goddesses

    A.   Hera

    B.   Aphrodite

V.   The goddesses' assertion of power

    A.   Hera

    B.   Athene

SECTION FOUR

Bibliography

Quotations from the *Iliad* are taken from the following translation:

Homer. *The Iliad of Homer.* Tr. Richmond Lattimore. Chicago: The University of Chicago Press, 1951.

Other Sources:

Homer: A Collection of Critical Essays. Ed. Robert Fables and George Steiner. Englewood Cliffs, N.J.: Prentice-Hall, Inc., 1962.

Homer's The Iliad: Modern Critical Interpretations. Ed. Harold Bloom. New York: Chelsea House Publishers, 1987.

Michalopoulos, Andre. *Homer.* New York: Twayne Publishers, Inc., 1966.

Murray, Gilbert. *The Rise of the Greek Epic.* New York: Oxford University Press, 1960.

Sheppard, J.T. *The Pattern of the Iliad.* New York: Haskell House, 1966.

Vivante, Paolo. *The Iliad: Action as Poetry.* Boston: Twayne Publishers, Inc. 1991.